Find The Guide Inside

A Path To Liberation

Garin Zina

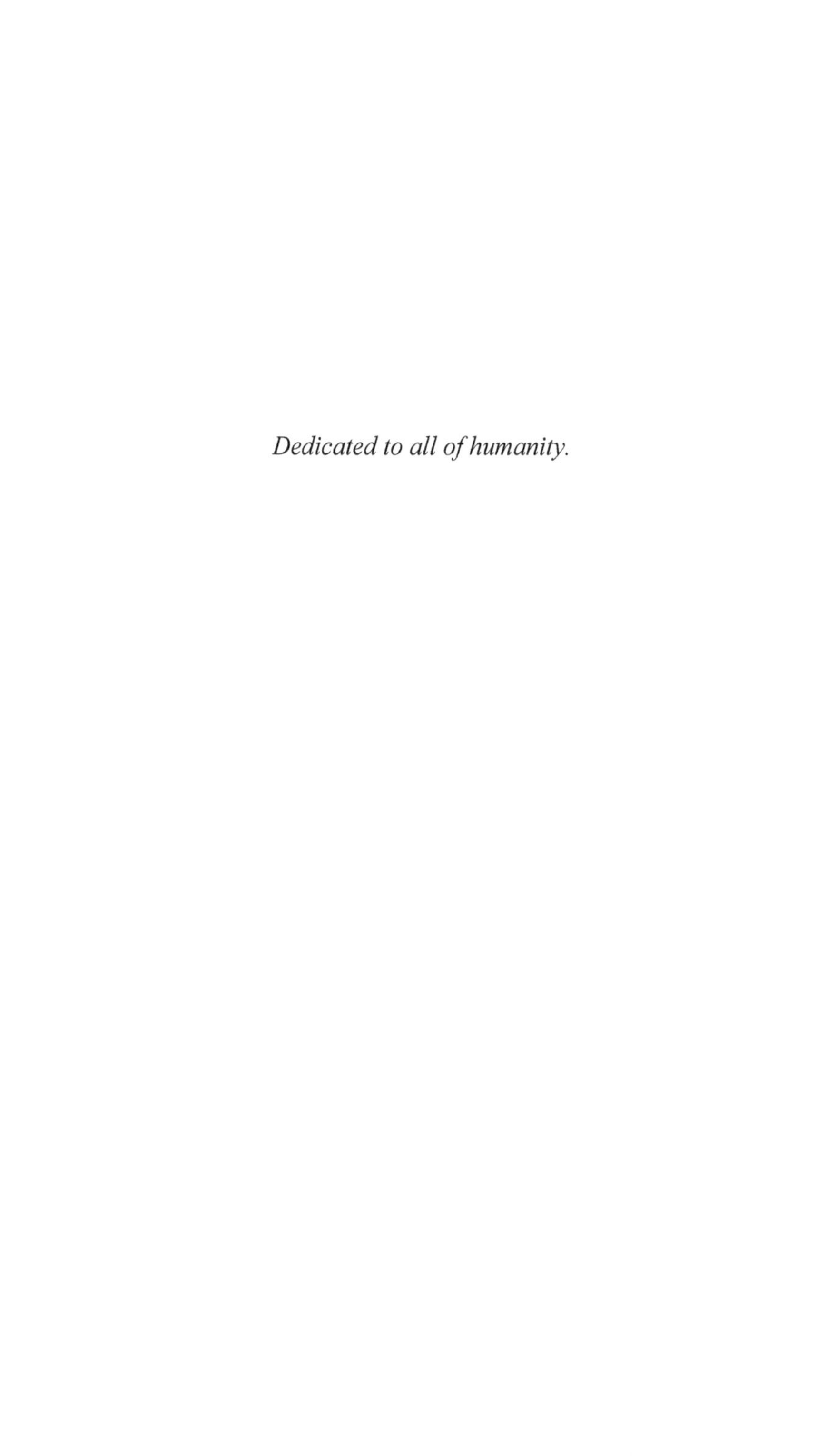

Dedicated to all of humanity.

Contents

Preface — vii
Letter from the Author — ix
Introduction — xi

1. The Illusory Mind — 1
2. Time — 4
3. Balance - Light and Dark — 7
4. How This All Ties Together — 9
5. Brain — 11
6. Seeding - How Change Happens — 13
7. Shadow — 16
8. How To Face Your Shadow — 19
9. The Emotional Guidance System — 24
10. The Most Powerful Guide: Direct Question and Answer — 26
11. Question Hacking — 29
12. Direct Link To The Guide — 31
13. Question Seeding — 34
14. Twins of Fate & Destiny: Serendipity and Synchronicity — 36
15. Active Miracleworking — 39
16. "Intuition is Intuition with the soul." — 41
17. How To Cheat The Maze: Reverse Problem Solving — 46
18. Inner Child — 50
19. The Disgusting Beauty — 52
20. The Eternal Law of Attraction — 54
21. The Supreme Law of Balance or Karma — 57
22. The Law of Sympathetic Resonance — 60
23. Enough Mystical Mumbo Jumbo — 62
24. Life Is Meant To Be Lived - So Live It Everyday! — 65
25. The Mystery — 68
26. Smart Investing and Spending — 71
27. The Balanced Way — 74

28. The Rare Few   77
29. Knots   81
30. Soul: The Great Alchemizer   83
31. Faith   85
32. Rights and Wrongs   88
33. Why does the Eagle soar?   91
34. Hunger/Desire   93
35. Joyslayer   96
36. Why Intuition?   99
37. The World's Best Boss   101
38. The Father of Lies, Satan Himself   104
39. The Blind Watcher   106
40. The Sun Will Come Up Tomorrow   109
41. Why do Humans have such a propensity
    towards Addiction?   113
42. Sundrops   117
43. We Want, but hate ourselves for Wanting   120
44. A Vial of Vile Poison   123
45. Acceptance, True Acceptance   125
46. God Of Perception   127
47. Time Flies When You're Having Fun   130
48. Anamnesis   134
49. How In The F**k Do We Do That?   141
50. Once More, How The F**k Do We Do That?   145
51. There Is Nothing I Am Fighting, Not Even
    Myself   151
    Epilogue   155
    Appendix   161

Preface

With my sincerest expectation of your positive experience I offer this book to you as a signpost in the middle of the strange world we currently live in. I am not right. I am not wrong. I do not know better than you. I just know what I know, help how I can, and do the best I can.

We all grow old. We all die. We all learn and teach and fail and fail and succeed, and only through sharing our fruits do others benefit from them. It is said that: "Society grows great when **old men plant trees** whose shade they know they shall never sit in." - Greek Proverb. I believe this to be the case regarding Wisdom also.

It is greedy to learn and not seek to help others learn. I plant seeds for the future in the present. I do not care if they are uprooted or if the tree lasts a thousand years, I care that I planted the seeds in the first place.

Read on with childlike curiosity as if you have just discovered a new toy or game, go on with fresh eyes, cleansed *doors of perception.*

I teach nothing new, I simply put it in different ways and look at it from different angles.

I ask strange questions and do not fear if what is being asked for is too much.

I look at the Truth even when the easier way out is to just stop and give up.

I, like you, am Guiding myself, and I, like you, am on a journey.

So do not hurry through this book, but don't be afraid to take the first step. As I have, in bringing you this offering.

Letter from the Author

"Emptiness is incurable, purpose is unfindable and happiness is impossible." That is the world's logic. For this world is a world of hunger and seeking to satisfy those hunger's. To feel whole is an impossible task physically.

You will feel the greatest poison of all during your last breaths on your deathbed - regret. The taint of a life unfulfilled, for like an empty shell, the life you created was passed by the world.

Desperate, the person lives for the future, worrying about the present, hiding from the past. Empty, the shell walks until it cannot hold itself up anymore and collapses, and at the lowest moment, a reservoir of strength is found, from an unknown space, a feeling on the inside.

Some call it God, Spirit, the Subconscious, the Universe, but whatever it is, it's really within you, and you it.

To remember this part of your Self, is to fulfill all hungers of the Soul and reunify with the most ran from place, the present moment, Now.

This book is unique, and not. I do not teach anything new. The Doaists thousands of years ago knew it, the Buddhists know it, the Hindus especially know it, Nikola Tesla knew it, David Goggins knows it and just about every successful person ever knew it in some way or another.

It's no secret, it's just You. But see with our schools, house, and work environments we have outside input, more specifically the sort of victim minded input that is spread like a plague and it is far scarier than Covid-19.

So stated simply: My great work in this book is the great work of convincing you, that You are You, and not the little you, the world and people try to convince You You are.

I am no messenger, prophet or teacher. I am a toddler in the eye of a cosmic hurricane we call the Universe, just like you. I have no clue what is right or wrong, and do not claim to. I do not know who should be in power or what we, as humans, should do, but I know what I should do.

And the thing that I should do that would be of greatest service to you and yours and my whole massive human family, is to stay connected to the high place of faith or belief inside myself. (I introduce you to You. Say hello to the Guide Inside.)

I present to you, the wonderful Guide Inside, You.

Congratulations on listening to yourself and following your intuition and trusting your gut to look at this. This is just a beginning, watch as the seed grows.

Thank you, "I love you like I love myself, because you are me."-Unknown

We are so blessed to be alive right now, more than we can comprehend.

And without further adieu I present this magnificent and shorter than expected great work, may your heart of hearts reawaken and live once more.

Introduction

How do you know you are lost, if you do not try to find a way out?

I feel rather perplexed sometimes when I think of the grand scheme of things. Life is so complex with so many simplicities that weave together and birth complexities. A an endless self-assembling repetitive maze of new forms and new shapes and sizes to ignite and capture my interest (distract myself) and momentary awareness and this *Maya* (Sanskrit for Illusion, referring to the Physical Outer World) is infinite, it is an illusory veil, and something to transcend.

As the grandeur of life mesmerizes the many, how does the one who sees far understand how to navigate in such chaotic waters? How does one know where and when to step? Where to go?

Intuition.

If and how, when and where are the details that fill in afterward. The future is a thing of **Whys**, an ever evolving self-stacking compendium of all cooperative components, the future is built on **Why**. People do things for specific reasons, *there is always an Intention behind people's actions*. The **Why** is a combination of *Intention* and *Emotion*. The waters that guide the future are *Intention* and *Emotion*. Many have diabolical *Intentions* while others bask in the beauty and blissful pleasure of ignorance. Many have honorable, redeemable *Intentions*, some seek to change the world, others seek to enslave it.

Couple the *Intention* to change the world with a burning passion and love for humanity and you now have an admirable **Why**. An Intention for a world enslaved and absolutely controlled coupled with a burning Hatred and Envy will plague a planet and create major unrest, and would be an entropic **Why**. Fortunately we can learn the lessons of past atrocities and not seek to *Intend* such torment on present/future cohabitants.

Now this is what it comes down to, the first step to navigating these waters with certainty and intention is a bedrock foundation **Why**. This is a self discovery process and is unique and different for every person who tries it.

My greatest **Why** is a hope to one day see a different world full of balance and peace and yet still thriving in novelty and ingenuity. I love the idea of a healthy humanity in balance with nature and themselves. A humanity where we know the past and also know our capabilities in spirit. A humanity where we are gifted with wisdom and grace and tolerance for others systems. Where people can always be kind to others, not because it is not kind to do unkind things but because it is natural to do lovely things. There are many more reasons to this Why and it is not limited to this, but this is a start.

No one person will have the same *Why* and that is perfectly okay.

Dive deep within yourself and find what motivates you, on a primal level, what makes you want to live, what inspires you to get up and move every day, what motivates you to strive for greatness, what pushes you past your limits, what makes you want to achieve more, what is the driving force behind you and your mission. Find it, RIGHT NOW!

Ask Yourself These 10 Questions and Write Them Down.
(This is the only part of the book like this)

1. **What is it I DON'T want in life?**
2. **What is OPPOSITE to what I DON'T want in life?**
3. **What Do I Love?**
4. **What would I give my Life for?**
5. **What holds me to this Earth, why am I alive?**
6. **Why would I care to care?**
7. **What is it that I really am afraid of losing?**
8. **What is my Dream?**
9. **What would I do if Money weren't a Problem?**
10. **Why do I think I have a shot at this life thing?**

Example Fill In

What is it I DON'T want in life?

To fail and never succeed and be stuck at the same job my whole life, to never have kids and die a lonely old person, deprived of all social interaction waiting to die to finally be released from your suffering?

What is OPPOSITE to what I DON'T want in life?

To score at Life in my 20s and find Passion in the work I do and be able to Do what I want, where I want, when I want, with a beautiful partner and create a vast amount of positive change on the planet.

What Do I Love?

Myself, my partner, my Family, my friends, my hobbies, my vices, my memories, my pets, etc etc.

What would I give my Life for?

My Country, my Family, my People, humanity, a religion, or an ideal etc etc.

What holds me to this Earth, why am I alive?

I want to live my life to its fullest and die a happy old person. Something like that.

Why do I care to care?

Because people that Love me would be hurt if I stopped caring, I would be a numb robot like a half sleeping/semi-dead person just walking around hating my own existence.

What is it that I really am afraid of losing?

My job, my security, my family, my money, my freedom, my choice, my voice, my friends, etc etc.

What is my Dream?

I want to invent something that will change the whole world.

What would I do if money weren't a problem?

I want to invent something that will change the whole world. And I would teach and vacation and buy and play and have a wonderful life.

Why do I think I have a shot at this life thing?

I think that I'm here because against all probability my soul got chosen out of the jackpot of sperm to be a prime example of how miracles are possible, and I can achieve anything; or if you're dark, something more sinister, like I'm here cause God wants to Punish me would work.

What we are currently doing is narrowing down your current view on you and your place in your life. See how you are allowing or sabotaging your results. Find all places where you are sabotaging yourself or holding yourself back or doing anything that isn't something you want to do long term. This is the hard part. Let it go, change, rewire, or replace it with something healthy, beneficial, or something allowing more success.

From asking the above questions you are one step closer to finding your *Why*. Once you find your *Why* you can then learn how to be guided by the insight of your Soul - Intuition, which is **The Guide Inside** on how to actualize your *Why* and bring it into the world. The Intuition will give you your golden nuggets or full roadmaps depending on how well you know your *Why*. It is absolutely crucial that you know Yourself, for no one else is you and only you can complete this process.

You begin Now, to embark on a beautiful and fiery journey where you will encounter many Illusions and False Beliefs that you no longer need. The false and sabotaging beliefs will be revealed and from that moment on you will willingly tredge forward to burden and toil from not letting go, or you will surrender yourself into the fire of self discovery and be reborn akin to the Phoenix.

Chapter 1
The Illusory Mind

"Like two golden birds perched on the

Selfsame tree,

Intimate friends, the ego and the Self

Dwell in the same body. The former eats

The sweet and sour fruits of the tree of life

While the latter looks on in detachment..."

— excerpt from *Mundaka Upanishad*, "Two
Modes of Knowing," Part III.I

Insecurity is a powerful driving force in the majority of minds these days. Images and façades are **Whys** unintentionally more often than not. (Wanting something just for the recognition or validation) An image to protect and fortify a chink in our emotional armor (from past trauma/pain). We can't stand the fact that some people are just "better" than us, faster, stronger, prettier, smarter, cooler than us. We lose ourselves in an endless chase and competition in which the only competitor is Ourselves and through our cognitive dissonance (inability to accept something outside our current belief system) we make out the world to be our enemy, to numb the pain of admitting our own shortcomings to ourselves. It's important to be raw, truthful and real in an inauthentic world.

Real is but a dream floating in the far distance to be glimpsed by those strong enough to rise above cultural fitting in. Truth is damnation for those who cling to illusions. Rawness is the courage to be authentic and genuine to the tee, unforgivingly and compassionately. Truth is a thorn in the eye of the Beholder because of its elusiveness. Many lose themselves in finding themselves, strange that the journey of self-discovery always ends back where it started, Present To Itself. Aware of Being Aware.

The ego is a self-protective mechanism, a faithful mirror, its only task is to remain constant to its view of itself. Rather contradictory as we are creatures of evolution, and so the question needs to be asked, since the ego always wants to cling to its image (meaning: if you see yourself to be smart, you will make a fool of yourself trying to prove to others that you are smart) then what is the true intention of the ego? It seeks Salvation in things outside of itself, it thinks that through clinging to an idea, or a view or a perspective or a way of expressing or being right, it will be safer and more secure than before. It is a King terrified of having his crown ripped off his head and so he death grips the security and in turn suffocates potentiality, unintentionally creating self-sabotage.

Unknowingly, the many fall prey to the game of One-Upman-ship and see that if they become better than the world or cooler, or more of this or that, then they will feel better then and be able to escape their current suffering. For this reason the Ego is vastly powerful in most people's lives. It protects them from The Unknown, issuing in a false sense of Salvation from the current suffering being experienced, and so an illusion is conjured up in your mind as a false belief or something comforting to keep you from changing your self-image and causing yourself more "suffering".

For this reason it is rare for the modern human to escape the grip of the negative Ego, always seeking to remain constant to itself and always sabotaging change if it feels uncertain. Now you can see why you must ask yourself questions to discover the Bandaid Self you created to not have to face your true self and to be able to see your *Why*.

Most people never even get to see their *Why*, with mild exceptions of moments of great achievement and accomplishment like graduations or inspired moments. Through the Illusory Mind or Ego the many never even get the chance to succeed or fail, because they never knew there was even a race.

Chapter 2
Time

"The Wheel of Time turns, and Ages come and pass, leaving memories that become legend. Legend fades to myth, and even myth is long forgotten when the Age that gave it birth comes again."

— Robert Jordan

The serpent of time that consumes itself is known as Ouroboros, represented as a snake biting its own tail, showing the wheel of time. All is Now, the great present moment. All happenings are experienced in a Now Moment. The Now is Infinite, Eternal and Everlasting. The state of being in which the *Why* is realized is outside of time. For time is an Illusion, manmade, and is maintained through suffering, which is in the mind. Ego takes many forms and through the suffering of duality (being trapped in the Ego or Illusory Mind) the perception of Time is created. To clarify, you stop experiencing the present moment and start projecting your mind into the future, or into the past.

Time is the separation of flow in the moment and suffocation by thought and analysis. The natural flow of things is Now. All flowing interconnectedly and simultaneously, in one massive ground of being, we call this the Universe. Everything is instinctually flowing with a subconscious and automatic precision.

All things happen for a reason, and yes the argument of "But why does that child have to suffer?" comes up, and listen, I'm no New Age everything is Love and Light promoter, which on a subatomic particle level is true, I am a promoter that life on this planet is both beautifully blissful and unique, but it also has its horrid, vile and filthy moments. We have contrast, we have duality. Balance is Law, All is One.

We are archetypal beings, our history is preserved in our imaginations. We have certain roles we instinctively fill, and out of "fate" or "destiny" we are dragged to be in the perfect place at the perfect time. Do we have universal forces pushing and pulling us from the other side? Do we have a higher version of us that is not physical that knows the Future, and guides us through intuition or gut feelings? I am here to propose that Time is the barrier between thought and reality. This is no new concept.

More importantly, Time is the experience of separation of what is and what is becoming. In order for the image or thought-form in the mind to make it out onto the big screen (life) we need Time for the cooperative components to assemble to provide ease of accomplishment. You see, Time is always on your side, right when you think you're gonna be late because you miss a turn, you see a sign for a detour and it leads right to where you need to go.

Time is fate pulling you along to your own creation. If you are to evolve, and change, you can only presume that your environment has to change as well, and so Time is the experience of evolution of Self and Environment. Inner world and Outer. Yin and Yang.

Chapter 3
Balance - Light and Dark

"Know ye, that all space is ordered. Only by order are ye One with the All. Order and Balance are the Law of the Cosmos. Ye shall be One with the All."

— Emerald Tablet of Thoth (Tablet IV, the Space Born)

We live in a Dual universe, an innerworld and an outerworld, an Objective and Subjective, a Divine Masculine and Divine Feminine, Left Brain and Right Brain and finally Yin and Yang. Through contrast and duality (good and bad) we have the opportunity to have human existence and experience. Without rainy days how do we appreciate the sunny ones?

If one only knows luxury, what luxury do they have at all? Through lack and having we can have extraordinary lives. Just as Alan Watts always talks about, if you could dream any dream at night, you would do everything in the Universe eventually because you would expand Time to feel like an 8 hours' sleep is a lot longer in dream time. And through doing everything and having anything you'd eventually get bored, and so you wanted some novelty, a nice surprise, so you erased your memory and flung yourself down to Earth. Welcome to the party, this is where the fun begins.

Chapter 4
How This All Ties Together

"Not all those who wander are lost."

— J.R.R. Tolkien

The reason we need to know about our **Whys** and our Illusory Mind (ego) and the nature of Time and Duality is because in order to Find The Guide Inside, we must:

1. Discover what we want or where we want to go with our lives (or an idea of it),
2. See where we are in relation to where we want to be,
3. Heal our limiting beliefs by:
4. Processing our emotional pain and trauma that caused the beliefs,
5. Adopt new desired beliefs opposite to limited beliefs,
6. Practice new habits and ways of thinking and acting that promote new desired beliefs to form.

By doing all of the above we create the perfect mental and emotional "environment" to help us bring our **Why** into the world. By having a vision or image in your mind of how life

COULD be (by knowing your *Why*), you create a bridge between your Conscious Mind and Subconscious Mind, and with this fusion, ideas and insights and nudges and feelings and "gut" feelings and all different forms of Intuition will come to you in ways you simply cannot fully comprehend. And they will guide you on how to accomplish your *Why*, every small step you take on this journey is a part of your Soul's Grand Plan for you, and the Guide Inside is just waiting to help you accomplish it. The guide to me is Intuition, for some it is God, for others it is their "guardian angel" and in the end, in God's universe, all the different words we use describe the same thing: tapping into Spirit.

Chapter 5
Brain

"I wanted to change the world. But I have found that the only thing one can be sure of changing is oneself."

— Aldous Huxley

This is how I believe that Intuition functions within the brain. I'll keep the boring stuff short and simple (sort of) . We have roughly 100 billion neurons in our brain, each neuron is like a small moving root network and connects to 10,000 other neurons and they connect to 10,000 more and so on to create "neural paths", each neuron is receiving and transmitting electrochemical signals through to their neighbors. Similar to how wires have insulation around the copper inside, neurons have a white fatty substance around them "insulating" them. This substance is called myelin, made up of countless cells called oligodendrocytes that form a wrapping/sheath of sorts around the neuron. If myelin is taken out the neuron's electro-chemical signals disperse into surrounding tissues or cells. In a strange sense information drips out.

As we age a layer of myelin forms and "insulates" each neuron. When we are young we have less myelin, and so from having less "insulation" for our neurons, we have more information traveling and dispersing through the brain. Which is speculated to be the cause of childhood dream worlds and extra vivid imagination. I will tie this all together further on. We've all heard the phrase "we only use 10% of our brain power", the reason for that is because we have a cell type in the brain called glial cells that outnumber neurons 10 to 1, so effectively all neurons are only 10% of the number of glial cells that exist. Glial cells communicate differently than neurons, they have a wave that spreads out evenly in a circle from the center of the cell instead of single directionally like neurons. This movement is called the "intercellular calcium wave".

Scientist Andrew Koob suggests that calcium waves and glial cells are responsible for thought. Published in Scientific American in October 2009 he talks about the most abundant type of glial cells related to neuronal synapses, called: astrocytes. In this he writes "...in this theory, neurons are tied to our muscle action and external senses. We know astrocytes monitor this information [muscular and sensory neuron activity]. Similarly, they can induce neurons to fire. Therefore, astrocytes modulate neuron behavior. This could mean that calcium waves in astrocytes are our thinking mind."

The reason I am including this here is because I believe that if thought is "intercellular calcium waves" then intuition is concentrated information being dropped like droplets and spreading waves of "intercellular calcium waves" to other nearby astrocytes eventually to be interpreted as a "realization" or "knowing" and "blocks of thought" or as I like to say a download.

Chapter 6
Seeding - How Change Happens

"The journey of a thousand miles begins with a single step."

— Lao Tzu

Everything that ever was or ever will be, first was a seed, within the mind of God or the Universe. We have information being processed in the brain with electrical signals and so, by focusing on certain things or aspects of our experience, we are literally seeding new electrical structures within our brain. So if one person is happy in a room full of well-intended depressed people, the mentalities of the ones depressed will seed into the positive ones mind and vise versa (for example, if all you ever hear is complaints, eventually you will become a complainer). It's like seeds of hope, one small seed then becomes a burning passion and metaphorically speaking becomes a massive tree.

With insight from spirit/intuition or a nudge to be more careful during a time of possible danger, we are seeded with the thought of caution. Which in turn allows you to further seed all things we come into contact with during our lives. A seed can be good advice, it can be an insult to seed shame in a person, and if that person holds onto that seed, they will plant a wonderful garden, full of shameful seeds. All negative or positive self talk is seeding for your future. How you seed yourself is how you create your future.

Do you plant seeds of hatred and suffering because of rotten seeds you're holding onto since a past trauma? Do you seed lies into your mind so you don't have to face the seeds of Truth? Do you seed self sabotaging ideas, to comfort yourself and not have to leave the comfort zone? We all have done all of the above. This is important.

Seeds are everything, with your *Why*, you seed your future. By understanding that through conscious intention to seed more positive thoughts into your life, you can then have an overall more positive life. And so by having the desire to **Find The Guide Inside** we are seeding the possibility of forming a relationship with our conscious day-to-day self and our Subconscious Super Self, or Higher Self. By forming this relationship you can consciously be guided by the Higher Self via Intuition.

With this connection being improved even subconsciously right now, you are now forming new electric structures within your brain to facilitate more frequent Intuitive hits or downloads (realizations). And in a sense, bridging Heaven (above) and Earth (below) so that you are a receiver of the information you are seeking.

We are transmitters and receivers, all of us. We are seeded with new thoughts that are in resonance with our previous thoughts. Meaning if we are sour seeded individuals then we will have more sour thoughts coming to us. This isn't the end all, of course, for we can dig up old "seeds" and replant new ones. This digging up is called Shadow Work, or facing your "Demons". Shadow Work has two aspects: The feminine (right brain) and the masculine (left brain). Which is so wonderfully experienced as Emotion and Belief. Emotion being the Yin (feminine) aspect of feeling and the Belief being the Yang (masculine) aspect of thinking.

Chapter 7
Shadow

"Whoever fights monsters should see to it that in the process he does not become a monster. And if you gaze long enough into an abyss, the abyss will gaze back into you."

— Friedrich Nietzsche

Due to humans inability to connect the dots looking forward, we have the propensity to live in the past, we become possessed by our traumas and see the world through the lenses of the past. If we are unable to accept and confront the emotional pain, we hold on to it. We will then be unable to change our beliefs, because of our inability to face our demons, or confront our shadow. We live in our pain body or a shell of a personality fractured and plastered with a false band-aid personality. If one faces and integrates the shadow. You then enter the Self. Once in the Self, you are living untainted by the lesions of the past. Of course it is like all hygiene, and must be maintained, if new work needs to be done.

There are two aspects of the shadow: the masculine shadow and the feminine shadow. In the end they merge and are simply the "Shadow" but in healing them we must see both sides. The Feminine side is experienced as suppressed or bottled up emotions, or traumatic memories and even small emotions that build up over a long period of time. And the Masculine is the belief you form because of those emotions. Because these experiences feel so bad while we are in them we block them out and try to "forget" about them. They always come back, but in a different form.

For example; you had a bad experience when you were a kid where you were ridiculed for expressing your genuine opinion (there are many terrible things that can happen instead of this, so I simply choose an easy one), so in turn you bottle up your true feelings and never learn to express yourself (you may have a belief like "I'm not good at expressing myself" etc. Down the line you will attract people into your life that will shame you for being you, over and over and over again until you face that shadow and pain. Accept it as your own and accept yourself. From having these small buildups and suppression of emotional pain, it will trigger you to form subconscious beliefs about whatever was experienced. This is the masculine aspect of it. Because that shame is suppressed, it's unconscious, and so a byproduct of that is a partner for the emotion which is the belief. Due to the desire to not feel shame in that way again, one will tell themselves something like: I'll never express my feelings like that to others again, I'll keep my mouth shut, I don't have to express how I actually feel, etc. After doing this for a long enough time and with multiple traumas, one will forget what it's like to be free of it. Once enough pain builds up, it ends up being a rude awakening.

Eventually once you dive into your shadow and feel your suppressed emotions and adjust your self-sabotaging beliefs you will have a clear and light time compared to before, though I warn you; once you start facing your shadow, it will keep coming into the light until it is healed. And just like all things, it requires maintenance. It's not a one-time practice and the world is "fixed" situation; it takes long and hard dedication, but the outcome is your true self, no longer fragmented.

Chapter 8
How To Face Your Shadow

"Memories are dangerous things. You turn them over and over, until you know every touch and corner, but still you'll find an edge to cut you."

— Mark Lawrence

I will touch lightly on how to face your shadows, as with all things in life, they are unique to your experience. There is not one correct way to do this, but this is a way. Be creative in the questions you ask if you are not getting the results you seek. Some may like to write this down or do it while in medita-tion, any way is the way.

Step 1: Fear

Ask yourself - What am I most afraid of?

What you see will not be pleasant. Once you have sat with your fears, feel the emotions that locked those fears into place. Such as desperation or hopelessness. Find the root of the fear and SURRENDER and just let go. Awareness is transmutation of the elements, from fear into fuel.

Step 2: Guilt

Ask yourself - What do I blame myself for? What do I feel guilty about?

Sit with your soul's burdens and forgive yourself. Allow any other emotions to come up and they will. Release them and forgive yourself. If you want to be positive, you must allow yourself to be, by forgiving yourself.

Step 3: Shame

Ask yourself - What are my biggest disappointments in myself or my actions? What am I most ashamed of?

Feel the uncomfortable weight of shame in your stomach and accept all of yourself, love all of yourself, even your mistakes.

Step 4: Sadness/Grief

Ask yourself - What am I sad about? What pain am I holding onto? What sadness do I hold onto?

This is where many are blocked because it hurts too much to care. Because to care is to feel and to feel is to suffer again. Be open to the fact that we are not perfect and must open our hearts to feel alive again.

Step 5: Lies

Ask yourself - What do I lie to myself about? What do I hide from myself? How am I not facing reality?

Confront all abandoned and forgotten aspects of yourself and welcome them in. See how you suppress and hide within your own psyche.

Step 6: Illusion

Ask yourself - What petty perspectives do I hold onto? What illusions do I hold onto? What do I not allow myself to face about life?

See that everything is connected, allow all seperate pieces to come together and see that everything is One. Even the big problems of today shall pass, and new seeds will be planted and grown. Let go of all illusion within yourself.

Step 7: Attachment

Ask yourself - What can I not let go of? What do I cling to? What earthly attachment keeps me from letting go of everything?

Fully surrender into the womb of creation and be at ease with all. There is everything in nothing and nothing in everything. Even these temporary forms we walk in are just shells of our true nature. We are energy and energy cannot be created or destroyed. Let go of this realm, let go of all you love, you will not lose it, but this is an exercise of letting go, an exercise of surrender.

All things we hold onto mentally, emotionally, and physically are just places where we can grow. We hold onto negative emotions because we don't want to have to live through them again, but in clinging to them, they cling to us and drag us into the pit we so fearfully run from. True power, true connection, true integration is the ability to let go. Once we let go of the negative emotions that formed all of these hiccups in our being, we can address the Beliefs we formed around them.

This is a powerful undertaking, many never even try to face themselves because they are afraid of the suffering they would have to go through in reliving their pains, but the beauty of doing this is that we no longer see suffering when we look back, we see lessons. Let go of your pain, child, wear it as a badge of honor if you wish, but do not complain when you lose faith in the world, because you lost faith in yourself first.

The power of vulnerability will bring you farther than any cold hardness or hatred, it will allow you to live within yourself and not be the enemy of yourself. The greatest enemy made in life, is the enemy never seen, yourself. Let go of your sorrows, let go of your fears, let go of your rage, let go of your hatred, be at ease. Let go of your dreams, let go of your hopes, let go of perspectives, let go of life itself, and soon you will glean the most profound thing you've ever seen or ever will see again. Yourself. Your true unchanging, unimaginably vast and infinite self. You are waking up from the dream.

This book is about **Finding The Guide Inside** and finding the guide inside, is about realizing that You (not your human body, but the thing underneath everything) is not your mind, is not your thoughts, is not anything conceptual at all, is not measurable and is not anything. It is the very awareness present at all times aware of being aware. It is the "ground of being", and consciousness of everything. In quantum physics, the wave (All of the electrons in the universe) is everything

and then when a part of the wave is in "view" it is the particle. Thus we are infinite and we are the collective electron
wave connecting all physical things in the Multiverse.

Energy is infinite and eternal. We are pure positive energy in
physical form taking on a wonderful and short journey. We
are given everything we need, with our own Guidance
System. This wonderful Guidance System is our human
ability to feel emotions. We are guided every moment by our
Emotional Guidance System.

Chapter 9
The Emotional Guidance System

"The emotion you feel is always about the vibrational variance between where you want to be and where you are. If you're out of balance, there are only two ways to bring yourself into alignment: Either raise your expectation to match your desire - or lower your desire to match your expectation."

— Abraham Hicks

Imagine human life without Emotion. Imagine dead eyes, and hollow smiles, imagine no care in the world to care for not caring. It is impossible to have humans without having Emotion. Emotions make us human, as much as we hate them sometimes, they are the fabric of what it means to be alive; Love. Emotions are a coin with two sides; Positive emotion shows you are in alignment with how your Eternal Self sees, and Negative Emotion shows you are seeing reality through the lenses of lack or The Illusory Mind (Ego). When in positive emotion you are in alignment with your inner being and when you are feeling negative, you are out of alignment.

It's okay to feel bad, in fact it's a great thing. It's a sign that however you are looking at the situation you are in, is not the way your Eternal Self sees it, meaning: There is always a more positive perspective you can use. When you feel anything negative, it means that whatever perspective you are using, is a part of the Illusory Mind or Ego, meaning in some way you think you lack something and so you are unconsciously giving into fear.

The beauty of this is that when you become conscious of feeling a negative emotion, it means your Eternal Self is focusing on the opposite of what you are currently feeling, meaning that all you have to do is ask yourself: I know what it is that I don't want, what is it I **do** want?

Let's say that you are driving to work on an important day and you see a sign for a detour, in turn your Illusory Mind will complain and try to tell you you're going to be late and your day will be ruined. If you believe that you lack time you have fallen into the Illusory Mind and will in turn create more lack; more problems getting to work in this case. If you see the detour as a good sign (as your Eternal Self does) you will soon be pleased to find your way through the detour very quickly and it actually leaves you with more time to enjoy before work. Glass half full or glass half empty, all your emotions will ever show you is whether you are focusing on the glass being half full or half empty. And that is amazing, if you think about it. Your own Guidance System to show you when you are helping yourself or when you are sabotaging yourself (and in the end even self-sabotage is helping because you are getting a lesson). Understanding that we are always being guided, step by step, every single day, down to the moment is one of the biggest steps to **Find The Guide Inside.**

Chapter 10

The Most Powerful Guide: Direct Question and Answer

"If you don't know, ask. You will be a fool for the moment, but a wise man for the rest of your life."

— Seneca

The mind is the most powerful supercomputer ever designed, whether designed or not the capacity of Mind is so powerful that any question we can ask, we will get an answer. Is the sky blue? Did you just answer that question without thinking? So you can see that any question that is asked is automatically answered by the subconscious mind. Why is this important? Because if you know what it is you don't want, you know what it is you do want.

Through the statement/question: I know what it is I don't want, what is it I do want? You get a positive seed to focus on. When you ask for what it is that you do want, you seed the possibility of it being real. So by asking questions you are forming a direct link between you and your Intuition or **The Guide Inside** (Higher Self). So ask more questions that seed more answers that help bring your *Why* into the world.

Say you've been having difficulty with losing weight, great! So the first step is to acknowledge what it is you don't want. We know you don't want to be sluggish, low on energy, unable to calm your appetite, flabby or flat out obese. So what would it look like if you were living how you want? We know you would feel energetic, thriving in your physical body, feeling light on your feet, like every moment feels fluid, with a nice body that complements your grace.

Did you know that in your Eternal Self or Higher Self is the balance between all opposites, and so your physical body can be represented by either or, neither is wrong or right, they just are. Through knowing what you don't want you will always know what you do want, you just have to be willing to focus on the positive or glass half full mentality.

Questions can be hacked of course, and you can "cheat" the system. One of the most important things to not ask is "How will this happen?" because then you will reignite the illusory mind and you will have excuse after excuse come up on how you can't have what it is that you want. You MUST ask *Why*. Once you know what you want, find your *Why* you want it. I'll use the above desire for an example question you can ask yourself. Why do you want to lose weight? I want to lose weight because I want to feel more alive, and I know that if I feel more alive in every moment, it will help my every interaction to be more uplifting and positive, I'll be more present, it will make me feel good about being myself and I like that.

You have to give yourself the thumbs up to answer your questions in a way that promotes more of what you do want. Balance is key, if you're a "debby downer", what do you expect? Sunshine and rainbows? Of course not! You expect an unfortunate sequence of events and badabing badaboom guess what's come to you.

Energy flows where focus goes, seed more of what you want, and less of what you don't want by asking positive questions.

Chapter 11
Question Hacking

"Judge a man by his questions rather than by his answers."

— Voltaire

What question would I ask right now if I wanted to know what I want? Ask the question that then comes up. What questions have I not thought of asking? Proceed to ask them when they arrive. How would I see the world if I had what I want? Visualize and feel the world as it would be. What would it feel like if I were to have what I want? Stimulate those Emotions, the whole "fake it till you make it" thing is real, just not in the way most people think.

If you have a legitimate answer to the question "How would I act if I had everything I want?" (For example). You wouldn't be faking it because that is how you would actually feel, so by embodying that state, you are literally seeding yourself into your future and bringing those conditions to the present. When you feel really connected to that positive vibe, consciously feel appreciation.

Appreciation is phenomenal because by its definition: "recognition and enjoyment of the good qualities of someone or something". You are seeding more of whatever is focused on.

So if you ask the questions to get yourself into the state of what it would feel like to have what you want, and then you appreciate the feelings you are having, then the insight and the realizations and energy are seeded, creating momentum in ways you cannot even comprehend. Because just in seeding more of what you want, you are literally rewiring your brain to seed more things, to be more positive and to ask more questions, and that's a lot of change. So good job at getting this far.

Due to humans being social creatures we can learn from watching. What this also means since you understand question hacking, is that you can learn from the version of you that already is living more of what you want. Meaning you are blessed beyond measure because of your Imagination.

If you ask the right questions to incrementally get you into that state, you can be aware of what it is like to be like that, and slowly but surely, you are adopting those characteristics and tendencies. Effectively seeding your new self. The key is understanding that there is no right or wrong question, no right or wrong desire, only more of what you do want, or more of what you don't want so give yourself a change and a chance, and seed reality from your *Why.*

Chapter 12
Direct Link To The Guide

"Life has no meaning. Each of us has meaning and we bring it to life. It is a waste to be asking the question when you are the answer."

— Joseph Campbell

We wax and wane as time moves on, and we recenter ourselves at peace. We humans, too, have cosmic cycles, like magnets, in and out. The Out cycle is of destruction and rebirth and the In cycle is of Focus and Direction. These two cycles mix as if two different liquids, swirling and intermingling around each other forever. This is yin and yang. These cycles happen everytime we breathe in and out.

As we integrate new information we destroy past versions of ourselves and as we focus and direct new information within us, we mold new possibilities into the mix. With each evolution and piece we are one step closer to the realization of our *Why* (your life dream).

Each and every moment is infinitely important to the journey, if you didn't suffer and learn the lesson, wouldn't you be doomed to repeat it? And akin to Tetris we build our lives and fit them together perfectly with our each and every response. If we chose one small thing differently, we would be a totally different person and would have a whole different life. It's important to remember that unless you seek regret. And now I have set the stage for the direct link to The Guide Inside.

The direct link to The Guide Inside is your Intuition, but did you know that every single thought or "word" you hear in your mind as thought is downloaded to you from your Intuition. As crazy as it sounds, and yes even your random thoughts, the crazy ones. They all are strategically "thought" to bring you into a certain state that will trigger you to respond to situations in a specific way. There are no coincidences. Have you ever asked for a sign for something or a message and then the random impulse to check your phone comes and you see something that correlates exactly to what you were needing?

This is another form of how The Guide Inside communicates. Sometimes we're too stubborn in the moment to see the sign we asked for so "destiny" or the Universe strings us along to some video or post that puts it right in our face. Some call this God or the Universe. It's all the same thing, the perfection of the in and out cycle.

We are given some form of situation or information to respond to, so we do, and then according to our response comes a new impulse, that impulse then leads to more situations or information to respond to and then comes in a new impulse, this continues until you leave this plane of existence. This is the evolve and focus cycle. Every piece of the puzzle counts.

And so there are some things we ask for that we are not ready to receive so we must be "prepped". So we are strung along step by step in the unknown until we find ourselves in a peculiar place - knowing.

Knowing, is the goal of this book, you can call it Instinctual Knowing if you wish, but the goal of naming this book **Find The Guide Inside** is for you to understand that there is a primal essence within you that knows what you do and don't know and guides you to further understandings that will put you in the perfect mental and emotional environment to Know. That is what **Finding The Guide Inside** is all about. The primal knowing we all have access to in moments of danger, can be harnessed and partnered with during mundane moments, to optimize your experience of life, to help you actualize your *Why*.

Chapter 13
Question Seeding

"The purpose of a storyteller is not to tell you how to think, but to give you questions to think upon."

— Brandon Sanderson

I hope now that an image of what **The Guide Inside** is is forming. Funny thing is it is something that cannot be imagined, only glimpsed. Though in rare moments you will directly see it, possibly in meditation. It is a force, something subconscious, the immortal Intuition we are all born with and are ever connected to. Through many experiments I have found that questions are a link to the subconscious mind. Now tie in question hacking and future seeding, this is how you can put your new abilities to the test.

1. Find something you want to improve in your life
2. Write down a goal for this thing/aspect
3. Ask yourself, what would I be like if my life were like that? Write down the answer.
4. Ask yourself, how would I feel if I had _______?
   (This is not limited to physical desires, one can

desire an emotional state as well) Write down the answer.

5. Ask yourself, what can you do right now to create more of what you want? Write down the answer.

Now that you have an image of what you would be like if you had whatever it is you want to create into your life, you can now keep an eye out for any experiences that show your change is happening, even the smallest changes.

Just be aware of the changes, in just acknowledging them and becoming aware of their presence will seed more change, then down the line when you see more change, it will seed more and more.

Everything in life is momentum, momentum is cumulative, and cumulative momentum is power. Harness your every moment to be in confirmation of your desired change, not to force it into reality in a "fake it till you make it" sense, but to confirm that the changes you are aware of that are happening right now are evolving, and those evolving changes will create more and more change that will drop you in the right place at the right time to show you that reality has become what you intended it to be.

Some may see this as wishful thinking, I see it as masterful thinking, for if you are not choosing your life, it is chosen for you. Keep an eye out for synchronicity and serendipity, brother and sister they are, and with them fulfilled desire is heralded. Gaze upon reality with a childlike curiosity and behold, what you have been seeking is right under your nose.

Chapter 14
Twins of Fate & Destiny:
Serendipity and Synchronicity

"I do believe in an everyday sort of magic - the inexplicable connectedness we sometimes experience with places, people, works of art and the like; the eerie appropriateness of moments of synchronicity, the whispered voice, the hidden presence, when we think we're alone."

— Charles de Lint

This is Carl Jung on the wondrous mystery of synchronicity. (He coined the term synchronicity) "A meaningful coincidence of two or more events where something other than the probability of chance is involved"

"That's just a coincidence!", "It was just chance!" I have been in too many places at the perfect time to believe in coincidences. Divine timing is law in a universe bound by cycles. Early one morning at the age of 12 or so I was with friends walking to the bus stop to get into the city. I had been told by the adult in the group to "stay in the back of the group", I complied. In the back of the group was my friend Jack, who had recently gotten a bad ear infection, so he could only hear with one of his ears. The main part of the group already crossed the country highway we needed to get across.

As I looked left and right to see if any cars were coming and I didn't see any, my friend Jack went before me, me a step behind him. Milliseconds later my foot caught on something and I tripped and took a few steps forward to catch my feet, pushing me ahead of Jack. On the left side of us I could now hear something in the distance. Keep in mind, the left is the ear that my friend had the infection in. All of a sudden I hear and see a truck barreling around the corner and my friend didn't notice. I jumped and caught one of his limbs and rolled backward off of the street. We narrowly missed being made into roadkill.

Due to the fact that Jack had been in the back of the group by himself, and I was in the front and then was sent to the back. I was able to be in the right place at the right time to save my friend from a hidden enemy he couldn't even hear. This is just one of hundreds of examples of divine timing within my life. Back in the early days of my Law of Attraction experimentation in 2017 (I have known of the great law since the early 2000s), I would ask the Universe for things, usually they would be fulfilled, but the most interesting of them is when apparent "randomness" is in the picture.

I used to work out of my friend's garage as a data entry clerk for a government registration renewal agency. I forgot to bring my lunch one day (randomness); I decided to say, "Yes I forgot my food, but somebody will bring me a pleasant surprise." and within minutes my friend comes into the garage with a plate of fresh scrambled eggs, looking oh so scrumptious, he asks me, "Would you like some eggs? I made way too much for myself."

So what? You may ask, things just happen, you may say, to justify a miracle and make it normal. There's nothing that strange, things just happen they'll say. I want to impart to you the inkling that reality is a gem, polished just for you. And on your beautiful canvas, are many coincidences unique to you. Subjectivity is key in understanding synchronicity. You may think a thought or ponder a memory and an instant later you behold the same thing in the "real" world. Whether on a billboard passing by, a song on the radio, or people "randomly" bringing things up. We are all interconnected, and the miracles we birth from unique beliefs, are the fruits of seeds long planted. Even recently planted seeds, if in the right mental and emotional environment, will grow to be big redwoods in a matter of moments if alignment is within thee.

The wonder of synchronicity is not the gift it brings, but the seed of faith and trust in yourself it fortifies.

Chapter 15
Active Miracleworking

"With man this is impossible, but with God all things are possible."

— Matthew 19:26

As the creator and guider of your life you have the wonderful opportunity to make life what you wish. If all of your experiences, sour and sweet, were for the single purpose of tuning you to create more of what you want, shouldn't you wake up ecstatic everyday? Shouldn't you behold every moment of your life as precious? Shouldn't you be more at peace?

The turmoils and batterings of life never fail to sequester one's dreams. The resilience of the ages is to reclaim your vision, and let loose the reality within. Duty is at the forefront of most minds, and the miracle of life is lost. The gleam and beauty of all things are dimmed, and suffering is the new language of love. The lessons of pain whether internal or external have one effect: change.

Change is the engine that powers the universe, some call it decay, I see it as rebirth. The foundation must be cleared for new creations to come. The glory of structure reaches its crescendo when form decays and all aspects return to their primordial source - potential. (When experiences fade into the past and you are left wondering, "what is next?")

Infinite, intangible and irrefutable pure potentiality. Infinity. Imagination. The wise Neville Goddard once said "Imagination is seeing with the eye of God".

All variations of all experiences of all conceivable and inconceivable realities lie within the great body of imagination. The vast ocean of possibility, ever shaping and guiding the collective destiny of all things, will always hinge on one thing - Intention. That is why your *Why* is so important, it is your current Intention, and in turn will be your fate.

Fate is a trickster that cheats all players in the game, willing or not, always delivering one thing faithfully - change. Motion is eternal, upward motion is deliberate and downward motion is self-sabotaged into being. All things happen in a form of Miracleworking. It is my wish to impart an Active Miracleworking frame of mind to you. For we share a common seat in this subjective cosmic play, the seat is of the director.

It is my sincerest desire to seed more Active Miracleworking into this world. And perhaps, one day, I will look back on this world, and think, "I have reaped what I sowed, and so have my brothers and sisters."

And that day, will mark the end of an age of non-deliberate creation, and will foreshadow an age of true and lasting peace and love (gibberish I know, but I believe it is possible).

Thank you for aiding me in this mass reconciliation of humanity's honor.

Chapter 16
"Intuition is Intuition with the soul."

"Intuition is seeing with the soul."

— Dean Koontz

Remember "Your time is limited, so don't waste it living someone else's life. Don't be trapped by dogma - which is living with the results of other people's thinking. Don't let the noise of others' opinions drown out your own inner voice. And most important, have the courage to follow your heart and intuition." said Steve Jobs

If all objects in the world first resided within someone's imagination, then Intuition is the vehicle that delivered the thought before it became a thing. All possibilities twist around an open mind, if rigid and too structured, all possibilities find a sweeping wave of negligence.

Blocked and bound, your mind will shun new thoughts and ways. This is the way of comfort. People think the comfort zone dominates the outer world, though it is more a thing of thoughts.

The Illusory Mind/Ego likes to remain constant, and so if one thinks they "can't" do something in their mind, then one won't do something. If one can see themselves doing something in their mind first, and believe in themselves, then they will do that thing, and a wonderful wisdom shows itself and the person opens up to the insight of the soul, downward streamings of Intuition.

If you recall the Brain section before, the cocktail of billions of neurotransmitters are employed as the bridge and bridge-makers of your informational processes, ever guiding you to your next decision. We make thousands of decisions each day. If only the choices we made could somehow be "fact checked" to be the best decision before we made them. Well they can, that "fact checker" isn't really a fact checker, it's more of a card dealer in Texas Holdem. You are dealt a couple cards of your own and then the group has some of their own, and so it's a collaboration.

Consider that each card that you build your hand with, is the information you need to adequately "win the game", now look at "winning the game" as making the right decision. To do so you have to be aware of your cards and their role in the environment (the visible cards they're paired with). You can only win the game if you see the value in the cards you were dealt, so you have to be open to the value of your Intuition, to better interact in your environment, and ensure you have made the best decision.

The next step is Trust/Faith in yourself. Once you realize that Intuition is present at all times, you realize that no matter what decision you make, it is the right decision, because it is a decision. Think about how many moments in your life would have altered your whole life if they were done differently.

This opens many questions about morals and ideals, such as, if no matter what decision you make, it is the right decision then was Hitler right? I am not here to tell you what is right or wrong morally (obviously anything that requires harming another human being to accomplish something is wrong and shouldn't be done), but at the most fundamental level free will is active in all decision making and the subconscious can't differentiate decisions.

That is a very controversial idea because people cling to victimhood, and think "How could I possibly create something into my life I don't want? I would never do something like that to myself." Well technically all forms of negative bashing inner criticism is doing that, all self-judgment, all self-condemnation, all worrying, all doubting, and all negative expectations are creating things "you don't want". Yet you still do it, even while knowing it isn't good for you.

Find The Guide Inside is about showing you that you glimpse or even see from the perspective of your Soul very often, and so from the perspective of your Soul (the guide inside) every decision is the right decision no matter what you do. It's important to <u>choose</u> integrity and to <u>choose</u> respect and to <u>choose</u> not to harm others, because that makes up being a "good person". Let's face, it in the grand scheme of things and through the eyes of sin, none of us are "good people", we all have our shortcomings and flaws, but through the conscious decision of actually trying to be better and intending well to others we can create more of what we all want in the world.

Remember: Treat others how you would like to be treated.

So back to Trust/Faith in yourself. When you make decisions in life they lead up to future decisions and those future decisions lead onward past the horizon of conceivability. (If you like time travel, call it the Event Horizon)

Recall that you can only connect the dots looking backward so the consequences of a decision you make right now can only be understood in the future when you are looking back, so you must and I mean must, step forward in trust in self. What trust and faith do is ensure that the outcomes of your decisions are aligned with your inner vision of imagination of what you want to happen. Now perhaps you can see why it is so important to know thyself, but more specifically to know your *Why* which is your Dream for life or your Vision. Without knowing what you want, how could you ever know that what you are experiencing is what you don't want?

The importance of trust in self is that it brings down Intuition correlated to your *Why*, one may even say, the Intuition is from your *Why*. Instead of thinking <u>about</u> your *Why* you are thinking <u>from</u> your *Why* or "Fulfilled Desire" as Neville Goddard puts it.

From and about are two very different things: *about* is speculation about the future and *from* is as if it already happened (or you already are it or have it, whatever "it" may be) and you are connecting the dots looking backward in time.

In using the infinitely powerful "Direct Guide" which is auto-inquisition or asking yourself questions, you can ask for answers <u>from the place of your already fulfilled *Why*,</u> instead of relying on pure reason and intellect to try and connect the dots of how to get there, you then harness quantum physics and are outside of time.

An example question for this could be, how would I act if I already had the confidence I wanted? You would be able to use your imagination to short-circuit your Ego and make it so that you can be different than your self image, and in turn see that it is possible for you to become something your mind tells you you are not. "What <u>Would</u>" is a very powerful beginning to questions, because it implies already being where you want to be. Remember this is about thinking/intuiting from fulfilled *Why*.

You cheat old Ouroboros the great serpent of time by dancing on its scales and shooting your Eyes forward in "time" to see what you have in store for yourself, giving yourself vision of what is to come, and allowing your creative ability to prosper in the seeding of your future you.

Chapter 17
How To Cheat The Maze:
Reverse Problem Solving

"People usually fail when they are on the verge of success. So give as much care to the end as to the beginning; then there will be no failure."

— Lao Tzu (Tao Te Ching)

If you know someone that is knowledgeable in life that is close to you, you most likely have heard of the idea of working on problems backwards (reverse engineering). In other words you fast forward to where the solution is already implemented and you turn around and look at the steps you would've taken to get there. This process has many different names according to who's teaching you; I'm going to call it Reverse Problem Solving.

You may have picked this book up because you have too many problems in your life and you want a nudge in the right direction. You may have picked this book up because you want a different perspective, or you may just be curious about what's inside, whatever the reason, you started reading this because of one thing, you were drawn to it. That attraction factor is like the ebb and flow of the tides of the ocean. Sometimes you go more inward and introspective, at other times you are outward and more of the world. In each of these there are specific benefits. With going inward, you see yourself and your life in a subjective way giving you more understanding of how to change it, in going outward, you see your relation to those around you and how you contribute to your problems, as an environmental participant, though the key is to be balanced in between. Be conscious of the inner world while participating in the outer world while maintaining your healthy boundaries to ensure you don't burn out.

When we have a destination in mind, which we do, it is your *Why*, we can see where exactly it is we intend to be. That is, what we want our outer environment to be, and how we want our inner environment to be, in correlation to the outer and vice versa. (What kind of life do we want, what life would feel the best). We can then put ourselves in the perspective of what it would be like if it already were and we would see from that distant point and look back on what it is we would need to become to actualize it. That's where Reverse Problem Solving comes in, working your problems backward.

Don't look at your *Why* as a problem, but as an opportunity. It's the opportunity for you to quantum leap and do a full 180 degree turn in life so to speak. So the first step in this process is really being honest in what you actually need to do to reverse engineer the steps to where you want to be, people expect having to do more to accomplish a little part of the plan, but what really needs to be done is people have to do less but the doing has to be more working smart instead of working hard. It's about leverage, using the natural flow and not forcing, getting more bang for your buck.

See the exact steps you would take, let's say you want to get a better job more suiting your personality.

First: You'd have to look at where you are internally (mentally and emotionally) and externally (physically) in regard to the job. Do you have the necessary skills to do the job effectively? Are you prepared for what is going to be asked of you? Are you knowing what you could improve on? Now remember that Gandhi said: "Be the change you want to see in the world." So by changing within, all things without (outside) have to follow in change.

Second: Change within and then act on the outside and the outside will change. Once you've sharpened your skills you can see that the next logical step would be to go out and look for that job but we have to remember the Reverse Problem Solving, so if you look backward from the problem already being solved, you would get the job then, before you'd probably be contacting any places that interested you to get a job there then, you'd probably plot out some time to go searching for a place in your area with vacancy, and even before that, if you know the niche you will be working in, you'd probably practice before, and before that you would update your capacities to entail what would be needed for the job.

Third: Understanding that where you are right now is the first step in the reverse engineering of your future, so follow the exact steps you see as correct to insure to yourself that the path you are on is just the path you would need to take step by step to actualize your *Why*. This scenario *Why* is getting a job that works with your personality (I've obviously shortened the process for time's sake and so you can do it on your own).

What this boils down to is: When you change inside, outside will follow. When you Reverse Problem Solve, solutions will follow. If you do things differently there is nothing else that could happen but different circumstances arising then you are used to.

Chapter 18
Inner Child

"To be more childlike, you don't have to give up being an adult. The fully integrated person is capable of being both an adult and a child simultaneously. Recapture the childlike feelings of wide-eyed excitement, spontaneous appreciation, cutting loose, and being full of awe and wonder at this magnificent universe."

— Wayne Dyer

There lies a flame hidden deep inside, dormant in most past teenage years, this spark is the inner child. Daring to imagine, spontaneous enough to dream and free enough to change. With the bonds and chains of belief and pain, most are lost within the game. Their characters mold to the environment, forgetting that it was the environment that was supposed to be molded. The vision filled child-like state of mind individual molds the world around them to be the sandbox they dreamed of as a child.

Sweeping a hand here, creating a structure there, the only hindrance is willingness. When the child gets bored it dismisses what is right in front of him/her to galavant off to some other project to sate its fleeting attention. You see, the adult and child are very similar, the latter enjoys its radical expressions, while the former condemns itself for its behavior. In modern humans the creative and imaginative self is repressed and suppressed. And in turn the child is shrouded and a mask of worldly hardness is adopted.

The unacknowledged shame of the adult is that it yearns for his/her past childlike curiosity and frame of mind, while still playing out the radical changes in attention. And not sustaining him/herself on any path, but rather seeking to find a path by jumping through many paths. The balanced mind seeks to integrate the shadow of the worldly psyche to uncover the long-lost treasure of the inner child, hidden beneath the muck of worldly desire. It is your inner child that knows your true hopes and dreams, it knows you. It is you.

Dive through your shadow and find the bedrock of your being, your Inner Child. See the gleeful moments where you shone bright with life. Those are your grounding stones, what was important to you then? How did you express yourself then? How did you see the world differently? It is unreasonable to ask you to stop seeing the suffering of the world, but it is not unreasonable to ask you to try to look at it in a way that allows a better future to come out of it.

What I am asking of you in this section, is that you grasp the lenses you once wore, and bring them back into being. Now you have seen much and can discern more, be at peace with what you have - you have just what you need. You now not only have knowledge of good and evil, but you also possess the seed of infinite joy and love, the Inner Child.

Chapter 19
The Disgusting Beauty

"Man suffers only because he takes seriously what the gods made for fun."

— Alan W. Watts

I am not in the position to say that all childhood experiences are meant to be, because how would I know? I have known a few people who have seen atrocities in their childhood years well beyond what most experience in all their lifetime. But what I do know is that, we all create our own lives, not from down here but from up there. The "up there" I am referring to is from a Soul level. If you could dream any dream, and you wanted to experience all things to gain the understanding of them, wouldn't you eventually take your memory away and put yourself in a more harsh environment to gain higher understanding from going through bigger lessons? Well that may be exactly what is going on here.

Akin to how a hermit crab goes about the world interchanging shell homes, what if the Soul goes about the planes and temporarily dwells in certain environments to achieve certain results. Wearing a new body here, living a different life there.This ties in with Karma, the law of cause and effect. Most view karma in the religious sense, a vindictive revenge machine that rewards the pious and smites the sinful. But I see it as something different. It is an imprint an experience has on you. Say you embarrassed yourself in front of class as a kid, when you remember that experience, you can still feel the emotion trapped through time. That is karma. The continuation of past energy that needs to be integrated, or in most people's perspective, Resolved.

The trap of this is that people take it to the extreme and become a servant to their karma instead of the maker of new karma. They lose themselves in finding the next thing to resolve about themselves, instead of completing the past through Shadow Integration, they seek to heal the symptoms instead of the causes. When a new You could be here right now. And the doorway to this you is: What would I be like if my *Why* were fulfilled?

Many expect the petty Laws of Government to change their lives and give them the leverage to do and have what is wished of them but there are puny written Laws, and then there are Universal Laws. These Laws are responsible for all things, all happenings, and all experiences of your life.

The Universal Laws I speak of are: The Law of Attraction, The Law of Sympathetic Resonance, and finally, The Law of Balance or what some call the Law of Karma or Cause and Effect. These Laws are irrefutable, unbreakable, because they are not a decree of man, but of cosmic cycle. These Laws will not be changed when wealthy bankers want to pad their pockets more or when petty officials restrict communities, these laws are Law, and cannot be undone, for Cosmic Law is Law. And this is where I take you next.

Chapter 20
The Eternal Law of Attraction

"An educated man is not, necessarily, one who has an abundance of general or specialized knowledge. An educated man is one who has so developed the faculties of his mind that he may acquire anything he wants, or its equivalent, without violating the rights of others."

— Napoleon Hill (Think and Grow Rich)

"That which is like unto itself, is drawn" That is the Law, the law of Attraction.

Let me bring you back to the Illusory Mind (Ego) section. We talked about how your Self-Image determines what you experience, and how when you hold a negative perspective about yourself inside your mind you will then see reflections on the outside to "justify" how you feel about yourself.

If you see yourself as ugly, people will come into your life to make you feel as if you are ugly; because "That which is like unto itself, is drawn" whatever you are, you attract. Be poor in belief system, and poor in physical you will be. Wealth is of the mind not of the world. Being rich is a state of being, not of accesories.

The incessant need and requirement for a victim is the perspective that life happens to you, instead of life happening from you. One will curse the faithful mirror and attack the reflection, when in reality all that it does is show what You are inside. Remember your most recent exuberantly happy day, notice how everything seemed to have a flow to it? Notice how things just happened right? There was a natural grace of unfolding to the events surrounding you, there shines a beautiful luck.Now I'd like you to remember the worst day you had recently.

I can bet that there was an unfortunate series of events, one may even say unlucky events that "blocked" you and "restricted" you. Everything felt slower, more bogged down, sluggish. Stuff just didn't work out, things fell and broke, people blocked you in traffic, arguments manifested and you got in your own way. You see, the state of being you are in has nothing to do with the world, but your environment/world has everything to do with the state of being you are in.

It would be naive of me to say that you are not at the whims of the world, though I dare to say the world is at the whims of human imagination. Every object ever created first was birthed in the curious minded individual's imagination and brought down through the Ether into physical form. We here in this physical world, are at the farthest extension of the Universal Life Force or Energy that creates all things, like the bottom of a funnel or in the eye of a storm, we are the center-piece of our individual universe. All creations happen in the ether or in the mental realms and are filtered into reality through the medium of time, time is the distance between one space and another; thus in time, the world will align to your vision. It is Law.

Chapter 21

The Supreme Law of Balance or Karma

"However many holy words you read, however many you speak, what good will they do you if you do not act upon them?"

— Gautama Buddha

"A seed is planted, a tree is grown, a drop trickles, the river flows, the Sun will rise, and will always fall, seasons change, fruit falls, winds are stirring, pushing all. The Earth lives, rebirth to All."

— Garin Zina

Just as the stars remain in perfect balance in the Heavens above, so do individuals' creations remain in constant balance with they're inner states. The Guide Inside always ensures you have what you need, and what you need is always inside. This is difficult for most to grasp, for they are convinced that the world of 5 senses is the only world, but this sensory world is just a shadow of reality. It is the farthest pushed out extension of the true world, the inner world. This inner world is the world of Imagination. Take a step back and note that all of your imaginings are the seeds of what you sense in this sensory world.

The fast moving blips we call experiences are just the momentary realization of something that was first within. As an apple tree makes apples, the Universe makes peoples, and these peoples dream creations into the world. On the level of Creation, when zoomed out to interface with, we see the sensory world as it is, Correspondent. As Above, so Below, as Within so Without, male and female, a light and a dark, no-thing and every-thing. We see that the world is not some random mess, utterly insane to contemplate, but it is by Law, created and corresponding to the Individual.

People will come up with a thousand and more reasons why this is false, for they cannot accept the fact that they create their own suffering, thus, illusion is born, and generations pass on in a sleeping state, only waking when they dream, and sleepwalking when they awaken. To pass on mentalities and beliefs to their future generations to perpetuate the comatose victim of reality archetype.

Everything happens by Law. To assume chaos, is to assume no control, and to assume no control, is to assume victim-hood. (Though to control one must surrender, so it really is a tricky thing)

Just as doctors try to cure "illnesses" (I put this in between quotes because many illnesses are emotional in cause) by treating the symptoms, they always fail, for the root cause is never healed, just bandaging the symptom so to speak over and over and over again.

The sensory outer world is just the symptom of the inner world. The inner world is the Root, or the Means to the End, it all starts inside, thus through changing inside, the outside will correspond. This is about waking up to the power of what "I Am" is, not "me" the little body walking around "me" but the thing inside you that you call I Am, your sense of self, that is the Root of all things, all physical and sensed things are just symptoms of the inner creation of I Am.

"I Am that I Am"

I Am is the eternal name of God, and the eternal resting place of who you and I are, it is the root of all symptoms, and the shaper of all worlds.

Chapter 22
The Law of Sympathetic Resonance

"If you want to find the secrets of the universe, think in terms of energy, frequency and vibration."

— Nikola Tesla

Earlier in the Law of Attraction section, if you are a question asking type of person, you may have wondered: If the Law of Attraction brings everything into my life, then how is it that the Law of Attraction determines what to attract? Simple, The Law of Sympathetic Resonance. Let's break it down nice and simple.

Sympathetic: "feeling, showing, or expressing sympathy." - Google

Resonance: "the quality in a sound of being deep, full, and reverberating." -Google

Sympathetic Resonance = Sympathizing with what is Resonating = Responding to what Vibe you have.

The Law of Sympathetic Resonance is the Law of Mirroring. That which you are within, is reflected out. Thus if you consciously draw Intuition down from The Guide, and have more deliberate thoughts, and guide your emotions more wisley you begin to have Reality respond to the higher Reality inside. All things that come into your life come from a place of mirroring, they always are corresponding to what you send out. So the big lesson to take from this is: Don't purposefully send out dark seeds when you know the seeds you plant today are the fruits of tomorrow, be open to change what you allow yourself to be.

Chapter 23
Enough Mystical Mumbo Jumbo

"The meaning of life is just to be alive. It is so plain and so obvious and so simple. And yet, everybody rushes around in a great panic as if it were necessary to achieve something beyond themselves."

— Alan W. Watts

There comes a point in everyone's journey where they realize that reading another book or article or asking another question or calling another friend just isn't going to cut it for what you need. You don't need more information, you need Integration and Implementation. You can always sit and dream about when you can control your life, and have what you want and can be what you want, but you're not gonna get there unless you Integrate and Implement.

All the things done in the world were done because the person who did them wanted to complete them, not because they read a book and got inspired or motivated. Ideas birth themselves, but drive, well that's another story. You can watch a thousand Youtube videos on how to manifest $100,000 to motivate and inspire you, but unless you come to a place where you NATURALLY think and walk and talk how you're "supposed" to, you won't scratch the surface of your Creating Ability.

It's up to You, to get your hands dirty, it's up to you to think deliberately and not be a slave of your Mind, it's up to You, to continue going on your path when darkness creeps in and forgetting and giving up seems like the only out, there comes a point in everyone's journey where they blame spirituality for all their problems and try to hide in a bubble of "that stuff's crazy". You try to forget and let go and "go back to normal". But when a can of worms is opened, it can never be closed, and you opened the can a long time ago if you're even reading this book!

So buckle down, get past your Dark Night of The Soul (If you're unfamiliar with that phrase, I highly suggest researching it) and revive your Mind, Body and Soul. You're not crazy, you just woke up, or maybe you're still sleeping? Maybe you're playing out old "programs" still, maybe you never woke up, maybe you never will, maybe you don't even know what waking up is, maybe you're just curious, at the end of the day out of everything you are or aren't, you're Enough.

Just keep breathing.

One inhale at a time,

So soothe the soothsaying victim-mind,

Awaken the Guide Inside,

And watch your life change,

As negative self-fulfilling prophecies die,

And self-affirming Dreams Arise.

Chapter 24
Life Is Meant To Be Lived - So Live It Everyday!

"Man is a microcosm, or a little world, because he is an extract from all the stars and planets of the whole firmament, from the earth and the elements; and so he is their quintessence."

— Philippus Aureolus Theophrastus Bombastus von Hohenheim (Paracelsus the Physician and Alchemist)

How many things around the world are happening Now? How many mothers are birthing new Creators? How many friends are having fun? How many do-things people are setting Intentions? How many kids are forming their dreams? How many Old Ones are letting go of breath and life and slipping away? How many Empires die each day? How many people listen to the victim beside them and ignore the champion within them? How many visions could never have seen the light of physical existence because of a naysaying family member? How many people strive to rise and conquer the winds, and bind the four directions of the compass in Union as Rulers or Politicians? How many die in upholding the truth? How many die for a piece of paper? How many people's inner child wilts away while the outer face of flesh mingles and learns the dance of the world? How many true selves never see the light of day, for fear of judgment? How many tormented souls never speak their Truth? How many people dance and sing? How many let loose tears in the breeze? How many lightning strikes are falling from Heaven? How many false histories are being written? How many Birthdays and Celebrations big or small, happy or sad? How many things are happening Now? All of them. All is Now. The Eternal Present Moment.

Life is meant to be lived, live it every day. Don't squander today for making up for yesterday. Find positive momentum. Live in mind, body and soul as a Whole Being. Live as your Inner Child, dream and fly in your imagination. Sign your sorrows away and adopt the ways of Grace. Grace is the natural pace of things. The cataclysms of today when zoomed out on are puzzle pieces and chess pieces that weave together new Nations and New Policies. Death is Rebirth and Life is Entropy. Life learns Death through Death learning Life. If Death is Rebirth and Life is Entropy, then Immortality and the place outside of time is both dead and alive, a synthesis of both, a transcendence of Duality and All Opposites. This Synthesizer of opposites is reading right now, watching, perceiving, experiencing, through you, we call this great synthesizer - Consciousness.

In Living right Now, humans bless and enliven everything else, for we are perception. If a tree falls in the forest, was it heard if there were no ears? We are the observer of the observed, we bring the Particle (anything observed) of Quantum Physics into awareness by observing the Wave Field (All of Space/Time Reality) and collapsing it, by virtue of our Observation. In order for Everything to be Everything, it needs to remain Whole, so in turn by observing any-thing we are making Everything collapse, and what we see and experience then is what we pick up with our Five Senses, this is what current Quantum Physics is about, roughly. In 2020 (the time during the majority of the writing) , the strangest year of all history.

Chapter 25
The Mystery

"To live in the world without becoming aware of the meaning of the world is like wandering about in a great library without touching the books."

— Manly P. Hall

Why are close to 8 billion people buzzing around working, eating, sleeping and repeating? What End does this Means achieve? Production. What kind of production? Multiplication of what already is. What is gained from this multiplied product? Expertise. What is born out of expertise? Innovation. What does innovation lead to? New Productions. And thus the consumer/producer cycle is born.

This has been the predominant path of life for most in the past hundreds of years. Find a job, work that job, get good at that job, create a new better job, get better at that, create new jobs or expressions of production. There comes a point where there's an uneven amount of consuming vs producing, and with this disparity, people become dependent on Consuming what is Produced instead of being dependent on Producing to

Consume. Monopoly is born and creativity dies for the mass herd.

A generation of consumers with hardly any produce, creates a lack of purpose and meaning. The Mystery of this here Age, is how to be in balance between producing and consuming. As you have probably just thought: How the hell do you do that? By deliberately aligning your every thought and Action with your **Why**. Your Vision, your Dream, the reality you want to bring to reality. This is your Seed, your production. In aligning your thoughts and actions and WORDS to this End, the only possibility is that it is Produced.

Let's change the word Produce to Invest and the word Consume to Spend. If you invest your words and thoughts and actions wisely, you can leverage your time to be on your side. If one only spends/consumes, then any reserves (of energy or money) are lost. Like an empty battery you stumble through life as a dead vessel, working against your nature, instead of with it, to compensate for the Spending, eradicating all possibility of being free to Invest once more. Locked in a cycle of compensation for lost/spent/consumed Energy.

We can observe this endless compensation for "bad" investments throughout all parts of life. A person is consumed (spent) by their shame, and seeks to compensate for this loss of energy by buying and putting on flashy clothes, to only get back a fraction of the energy spent, just to feel spent again, though even more this time. The person spends their Self-Love by basing their Self-Value on the conditions set by another person in a relationship (or love they receive back), and thus Love is spent and the heart becomes empty as the person seeks more and more ways to compensate for this loss. They spend time binging TV shows to fill the Hole inside of them. They spend time with people they don't like to fill the

Hole of not having what they want. When they want Love, not attention, this Love is impossible to find in someone else, if the fire of Self-Love has not yet been ignited.

For individuals are predictable, and thus the not Self-Loving Investor for Love, will spend and spend away, trying to compensate for the lack of self-love, and in the end only to dig the hole deeper, for the more energy and focus that is spent in compensating for this lack, the more one will continue spending.

See how Addiction has everything to do with everything involved in Compensating? If one Spends Energy, instead of Investing Energy, one will always try to spend future energy to try and make up for spent energy now, and in turn invests in spending. To truly be free, is to know the Mystery - Balance.

Invest so you don't have to make up for spending in the first place, Invest, so you are not a slave of your Past, Invest, so you choose what you want, and don't have it chosen for you. Invest, so you can be you, and not a shell of a person, slaving away to get back what you cannot spend again - Time.

Invest in right Now.

Chapter 26
Smart Investing and Spending

"Winners are not afraid of losing. But losers are. Failure is part of the process of success. People who avoid failure also avoid success."

— Robert T. Kiyosaki

That which is spent, is used, unreciprocal, and not returned. That which is Invested, is built, gains momentum and comes back. Spending is Death, Investing is Life. Two sides of the same coin, one cannot exist without the other. The crazed Investor seeks to eradicate all possibility of lost or spent energy. And like the King afraid of losing his Crown, death grips possibility and makes the outcome certain and rigid, and makes Returned Investments impossible. Investing and Spending both have to happen, but the rate at which you Spend, does not have to be greater than the rate in which you Invest. If done correctly all energy Spent, can be transmuted and leveraged as an Investment, though for this to happen Acceptance is Key.

The many ways that Spent energy is tried to be compensated for locks down potential for new Investments. Meaning, if you are stuck in the past, or stuck on Spent Energy, you will endlessly try to make up for something that is already dead. Like trying to resuscitate a long dead body. You must Accept past Spending to make the lost energy multiply itself, and come back to you, in the form of Returned Investment. (Similar to the concept of resolving Karma, people keep fixing the past while never Creating the Future)

The modus operandi for this is called Shadow Integration, and we have already looked there, this is just a reiteration of the importance of it. By Accepting the lost energy of the past, and integrating it back, a new blank slate is born. Your energy is clean and electric, and is ready to electrocute new Investments and reallocate past Spent Energy into new ventures, and new **Whys**.

All that ever was is dead and frozen in your memory, the suffering and joy of the past lives on in the halls of your mind. As beautiful and sorrowful paintings in the museum of your memory. These fragments are past Investments that failed, and were Spent, and if not handled and processed healthily, can bring back hauntings in the form of more spending to compensate for what you feel was lost. How many times have you seen that person with that bad habit from their past, self-sabotage their future and present, because they are convinced they need to do something a certain way, when in reality that Way of doing, was the very Spending in the first place that keeps bringing them back to the same issue over and over and over again.

If you don't learn the lessons of the past, you are doomed to repeat it. If you don't integrate your shadow, you are doomed to be Possessed by it. If you do not Accept and Account for past Spendings/Failed Investments, then you are doomed to continue Spending to compensate for what never was gained, and was lost in vain effort. Over and Over again, until the moment of desperation when Death is the only out, and your Self-Image shatters, and a new person is born, An Investor, an accountable person that learned the lessons of past failed Investments and moved forward with the Golden Seed, a blank slate.

Chapter 27
The Balanced Way

"He who stands on tiptoe

doesn't stand firm.

He who rushes ahead

doesn't go far.

He who tries to shine

dims his own light.

He who defines himself

can't know who he really is.

He who has power over others

can't empower himself.

He who clings to his work

will create nothing that endures.

If you want to accord with the Tao,

just do your job, then let go."

— Lao Tzu (Tao Te Ching)

Balance is inherently always shifting. As energy never dies, it only changes states.

This morning I found myself awakening to my alarm that I had set the night before for 6:40am. I planned to hit the gym for the first time in a while, since it had been closed because of COVID-19 and re-opened for the first time. During and after my workout I noticed how out of balance my strength felt. Normally when consistently working out, I have long muscle endurance, though because I had not been there in a couple months I was feeble and weak compared to "normal".

This showed me directly how, when we do things many times, in a certain way, they become natural, and when we do those same things during different circumstances, it's a completely different feeling and action than before. Obviously, we all know that when you don't workout for a while and you get back into the gym, it's a little humbling. That's not the point. The point is that, when we introduce new things into our surroundings or actions, we fall out of balance. In this case the "new thing" was less muscle. So why was it that I fell out of balance? Was it because of me having less muscle or was it something else? I think it's something else.

We fall out of balance because we have a nice system that makes us stay consistent with how we view ourselves, or at least how we think of ourselves. Once again this is called Ego or the Illusory Mind. Because I had not worked out in some time I fell more out of balance and noticed it more than I normally would because of the disparity between how I view myself (being a person who is strong and lifts a lot) and then being a lot more weak than usual. When we introduce new things or things outside of the normal spectrum of actions we take, we either take them head on and handle not knowing, or we cave in on familiar behaviors and don't adapt to change.

If I were a different person, a lazy person, immediately after noticing my weakness after a few workouts I would have called it quits, but I chose the option of facing the change head on. Which in turn changed how I view myself, which had changed from a strong, lift a lot person to a feeble and weak newbie, instead I catapulted into a new Momentum. This change of state represents many different scenarios. We get a new job and feel out of balance because we are no longer in the Known. We start a new project and feel out of balance because of being outside of the Known. We have to take over for someone doing something we never did before, we feel out of balance...

Always while doing new things, it will feel strange and out of balance from the known "normal" comfort zone. And always this can be changed by being open and present to face the changes head on while they are in front of you, before the procrastination or doubt thoughts kick in.

You will always have two choices: Go forward and Ascend, or Self-Sabotage and Descend. Lack or Have, both two sides of the same coin. Let go of fear of being out of balance and welcome healthy changes, or not, and fall deeper into the pits of self-sabotage. You always have a choice.

Chapter 28
The Rare Few

"Look at how a single candle can both defy and define the darkness."

— Anne Frank

Rare are the few who truly care. Rare are the few who know enough to care. And few and rare are those who seek to know. Rare are the few who are curious enough to know. Rare are the few curious ones and thus, we are The Rare Few who are uncommon amongst the uncommon, few among few, those who question. Those who seek, and who have ears to hear and eyes to see. All of us Rare Few are all working together, the system we form, the network we bridge, is forming many paths for collective humanity. And boy do we need it! We are connected and tied together as a species. It is vastly important that we are able to Synthesize our Intentions for the positive, if we are to create a favorable future.

It is rare for Modern Culturized Humans to want to face their fears and flaws, automatically giving the person a feeling of anxiety or a sense of impending danger. This is Fight Or

Flight, this state turns you from normal to stressed by turning your Autonomic Nervous System from Parasympathetic (Rest and Repair) into Sympathetic (Fight Or Flight), as you go through this change of state you will become filled with a chemical called cortisol which is secreted by your adrenal gland (where adrenaline comes from). Cortisol is the chemical that makes you feel stress, and all forms of negative feelings stem from this state, it is Survival Mode and it is *reactionary*. A wise Modern Human will always be more in *response* than *reaction,* because this is a dance, the dance of Survive and Thrive. Two states, Heaven and Hell, are both within our own biology, to show us contrast in life.

What does contrast show us?

It shows us what we don't want.

Why is that important?

This world is a world of energy, in what you don't want is also what you do want. Opposites. You know this when:

You answer: "I know what it is I don't want, what is it I do want?"- Abraham Hicks

This one question, this one piece, has guided every single human being for all eternity. The tears and sorrows of men, women and children, have come from creating more of what they don't want (lack) vs creating more of what they do want (having).

The little section right above this is cruel to the Modern Culturized Human, that believes that life is happening to them and is punishing them instead of life happening from them and for them, though in Divine Humor, your Soul laughs as you continually doom yourself to create more of what you don't want by virtue of *reacting* to what you created by focusing on what you don't want and so you now see and create more again. Consciousness is a cosmic form of a feedback loop, and so I advise, to rise, release your ties to Survive and rise above to Thrive.

All is created by Self. Self is no human word, is no image, no thought, no belief system, no reason, no power, no thing. It is what watches and perceives and births new things into reality. Self - Is creating by inhabiting and sharing Conscious Awareness and Presence of Now, within us. God, the Universe, All of Creation and Existence, is in your very structure and thus, since God made all, we too are God, or rather a spark and part of God. Though all of God is in us, our conscious selves, our Ego's and Minds, are not God. God is all things and thus must remain No-thing, for if it were concentrated on being one fragment of All-That-Is it wouldn't be All things anymore. It must be the Unity of All things. Thus God cannot be conceptualized or put into Form. And so we are here as the Eyes and Hands of God on a great farm, our Souls the farmers, our bodies the wheel barrows, and our Eternal Self, the garden. When we die our Souls have planted what seeds needed to be planted and we start another journey.

The Net of the Collective Subconscious of humanity weaves the Tapestry of all worldly events. As I am in Coronavirus month 4 while writing this now, 5/24/2020, I can see how the collective fear of humanity is welling up in people's deep subconscious and even conscious minds and is weaving a terrible potentiality. I seek, for the sake of all reality, to balance the amount of people creating what they don't want and the amount of people creating what they do want. Then the scales will change and Positivity and Higher Consciousness will be the new virus, implanting Inventor Thoughts and Planting geniusness and loving thoughts, forming life in a "I know what I don't want, what is it I do want?" (Choosing Deliberately what to create) kinda way.

The Rare Few, are those who create more of what we Do want. The others are no plague, they are hands and eyes too of the Creator. They serve a different purpose, no higher, no lower, just a different state, Survive.

Though right now it is rather hypocritical because we all are suffering and we all are surviving, it is an Ideal World if we can find a way to be calm in the storm and be Thriving, the inner kind of thriving. Not achieved by items or wealth, but the thriving of Creating and seeing that you can Create as an unchained person. Hand in hand Lower self and Higher Self weave the world.

Meditate on God, on Self.

Chapter 29
Knots

"Bondage is of the mind; freedom too is of the mind. If you say 'I am a free soul. I am a son of God who can bind me' free you shall be."

— Ramakrishna

Knots are funny. Knots are strange, the funniest part is we make knots. Not with rope, but in our lives. While not together in life, you may see many confusing jumbles and messes in parts or all of your life, when in reality, you have many Knots, many, many Knots. Knots of energy, blocked and constricted paths. Ways that don't serve your evolution any more. This book; Find The Guide Inside is about untying the Knots, and laying out the string how you want it, eventually to weave together a beautiful Pattern. A tapestry as I called it before. Look at your financial life, you see how you go one direction to start, then when the work needed to be put in comes up, you turn and change and start something new. That's a Knot. Untie the Knot by creating balance. How do you do that?

Take a step back and take an honest look.

Consider how you would've completed it had you already finished and done the task.

Do it, just do it, do it again, and again.

Give yourself rest time. Our bodies also need to be unknotted sometimes.

Find how to be unknotted in all parts of your life, find how to be Thriving. Not constricted and Surviving, Knotted and stressful.

There is power in balance. Not people power, or social power, petty power or even destructive power. This power is far more subtle, far more potent, more electric, life giving. This power is the Power of Creation, momentum.

Through this momentum new realities will be birthed and brought in front of you for your five senses to enjoy. This power is no joke, this power is inherent in All Things. One may call it the Universal Life Force, some call it Chi. On the energetic level it is an Electromagnetic Field.

This power is just an energy receiving field that reflects back what energy you transmit to it, via your thoughts, actions, belief and other various conscious and subconscious processes.

The key is to be Unknotted, to be loose and free of the binding of the Shadow. Shadow is meant to be integrated, not romanticized.

Unknot your self, unknot your life, do it for the sake of your own creative ability you don't even know what You have in store for yourself.

Chapter 30
Soul: The Great Alchemizer

"My brain is only a receiver, in the Universe there is a core from which we obtain knowledge, strength and inspiration. I have not penetrated into the secrets of this core, but I know that it exists."

— Nikola Tesla

For those of you who are not familiar with alchemy, it is the process of turning basic elements into different elements, for example: many Alchemists claim to be able to change Lead into Gold. (This is the outward appearance of Alchemy, when in reality it is all about spiritual transformation).

It is my Belief that the Soul is the Alchemist that brings our human lower self Animal/Primal nature and our Soul/Higher Self/Divine nature into balance and Harmony, and thus turns us from Lead into Gold.

The above process of course is overly simplified; what must take place is countless upon countless numbers of lives to bring the Soul to the point of Spiritual Human incarnation. Meaning, the Soul has had many upon many lower self animalistic primal nature lives (war lives, slave and dominated lives) that have led to a higher path, though in the eyes if the Creator higher or lower are the same, no better or worse, just different paths.

The Higher path is to Thrive, the Lower is to Survive.

Yes, always will one be in Survive at different points in life.

Yes, one will suffer and will not be able to get from A to Z easily.

Yes, difficulties will arise.

Yes, anger and hatred and fury may consume your heart.

Though, at the end of this dark night of the soul, this dark tunnel, the shadow integration, after it all, is a Light at the end of the Tunnel. It is You, Self, Immortal You. Your Perfect Nature.

Higher Self or Soul or Creator or Self or God, words are just sign posts.

You must Alchemize yourself to Know Thyself.

In Knowing Thyself, the shadow is integrated, the Self is seen, Higher Self and Lower self merge, and a new Intuition arises. A Primal Power, and Instinct, a flow like stream of power, the power of Creation. Prana. Chi. Life. Time. Space. Me. I Am. Energy.

Chapter 31
Faith

"Faith is taking the first step even when you can't see the whole staircase."

— Martin Luther King, Jr.

A rock sits at the bottom of a river, just as a person's faith sits at the bedrock of their being, as the waters of life pass them over. Over time the waters change, affecting the rock. Maybe one day the rock is a home for algae, maybe a century later the rock is clean and beautiful, though it is still the same rock. And thus Faith is Faith, not the thing you have faith in, but faith itself. The waters change infinitely as civilizations rise and fall, but one thing stays the same, Faith. Faith in what? What could one have so much faith in, that throughout the birth and death of nations they still feel faith? Faith in God? Faith in the Universe? Faith in Self? Or is it despair that is so faithfully focused upon? The creeping approaching death we all encounter? Faith that we will pass on and not be here anymore?

What we do know is that we all die. I'm faithful in that belief. What is dying? A change of state. And we base all parts of our lives around the 'before' death part of life, so what in turn do we have faith in? Faith in death? Faith in rebirth? Faith in the continuation of our species? Perhaps faith in ourselves? What faith bestows fear of the inevitable unknown we all reach? Faith of loss.

We all faithfully plan ahead and structure away our lives to accommodate the natural loss and decay all things around us. So we faithfully run away from the inevitable in vain hope to delay it or invalidate it. So on and on, we faithfully change ourselves and change our environment and mind and body to hopefully experience something different than what we faithfully run from. To arrive at the day where the faithful hound can return to where it came from. Unfaithfully changing the decision of the faithful little human to run and run from the inevitable, and now the only thing that can be faithfully acknowledged is Death. Why is death not acknowledged until it is birthed? Because faith costs one thing, life. For if faith is not had, then neither can life be, for what would life be if there were no Faith, but an empty shell of a thing?

The cost of Faith is life, because when you lose life, all that remains is the rock at the bottom of the river, the river being life, stopping for the precious possibility of Faith in something, and the reward is given, the reward being free will to have faith in anything, so that you may choose to be immoral, you may choose to be a King, you may choose to kill yourself, but you faithfully know the whole time, that it is YOUR decision, and faithfully you may decide, for either way one thing is guaranteed, your demise.

This is why the cost of Faith is Life and the cost of Life is faith, faith in oneself.

For Self, is all that there is, even in all the different "seperate" forms we all faithfully step forward in our in Faiths, as bedrocks of the rivers of life that we are, as we exercise free will, by exercising our Faiths and sacrificing our lives in those Faiths.

87

Chapter 32
Rights and Wrongs

"If only it were all so simple! If only there were evil people somewhere insidiously committing evil deeds, and it were necessary only to separate them from the rest of us and destroy them. But the line dividing good and evil cuts through the heart of every human being. And who is willing to destroy a piece of his own heart?"

— Aleksandr Solzhenitsyn

Too many people focus on What's Right and Who's Wrong vs What's Right and What's Wrong. It's a giant tattle tailing mess. It was him, no her, no it was China. Accountability is never taken, for accountability is impossible in the blame game. The blame game is all about Survival, all about the Illusory Mind, all about the lower self, a victim. What's Wrong? - is where the information is at, Who's Wrong? Is a dead end...We are all sinners, right and wrong mingling in one body. We have all wronged something and we have all righted things. No one ever wants to look at their own hypocrisy. Hypocrisy makes you feel a fool, and people don't like feeling a fool.

Feeling a fool makes you feel shame, feeling shameful leads you to do foolish things to make you feel better about being a shameful, foolish hypocrite, as we all are. We are not only this foolish, shameful version of ourselves, we are all states high and low, bleak and bright. Imagine that you are a person that has faced their hypocrisy and shadow and mildly balanced them, you would be a very honorable, honest and humble person, your head would be rid of pride. You would once more be open to learning; we get so caught up in being right, we forget to learn more.

We are shamed for our Wrongs and seek refuge in our Rights and we battle ourselves inside. One step forward to Right a Wrong, a wrong step forward, does this make you more Right? If a step is a step and Wrong and Right can both come from it, does that make you above Right and Wrong? If Right and Wrong are just two sides of your Moral Coin, then what really is Right or Wrong? What does it mean to be right? Usually being right means, saying a piece of information that is True, being wrong is saying something false or cruel. A word is a word, what deems it wrong? What deems the legendary Poems of the past "Right" in esteem? Perspective and perception, you deem it. Well okay, what part of you deems something Right or Wrong? A deep primal and instinctual gut feeling, that you just know, if something is wrong.

I know you know this is Right. So deep within you is a Compass, the most accurate of Compasses, but also the Compass most susceptible to interference from outside forces. These outside forces being strong emotions, impulsive self sabotaging decisions or any form of self-sabotage. Funny how I labeled the above as Outside Forces, if you notice, you're more likely to blame someone or thing outside of yourself for your own actions other than your own self, and that's in every situation great or small.

At a speech

"I am so thankful I made it this far, thank you God, thank you Mother, thank you Father." That is an acceptable "Right" acknowledgement to who helped you get where you are. What about when talking about a failure?

Talking About a Failure

"It's all their fault. The world hates me. That type of stuff just always happens to me. I guess I just have bad luck."

You see how blame during most failures is externalized and the world or a person gets Fault, instead of the only possible thing that could've caused it being acknowledged, Yourself.

To be Wrong is no Sin. To be Right is no victory. Only through realizing and accepting your Fault, will you be free to cast Right and Wrong as you wish. Though, do keep in mind that all Duality (Right-Wrong, Yin-Yang, Above-Below) is a part of the Illusory Mind.

To be free of the bonds of Right or Wrong, one MUST see from the Eyes of The Guide, or the Eternal Self, the soul or the Higher Self, there is a reason for all things, a ***Why.***

Chapter 33
Why does the Eagle soar?

"All the world's a stage,

And all the men and women merely players;

They have their exits and their entrances;

And one man in his time plays many parts,

His acts being seven ages."

— William Shakespeare

Magnificent, searching, probing the land. High above, the Eagle searches for its prey. It searches for its prey to not fall victim to natural selection or maybe just not to starve. Whatever the reason, the Eagle flies free, searching. It can find many different things, see many different faces, predator or prey, but in the end it is just free. Just free. A funny phrase that, "just free".

Many are "just free" and are in the worst prisons possibly created, the prisons of the mind. A maze to set your soul ablaze. With freedom comes choice, with choice comes outcome, and with outcome, comes pattern. To be free as is the Eagle that is soaring is to hunt habit and make it your prey. Kill and eat and recycle your old ways. Never and I mean NEVER let a pattern become a prison. For patterns multiply, and before you know it, you have a den of snakes instead of one little baby snake to deal with.

Don't let yourself be possessed by a negative pattern, but at the same time know when to choose what patterns are healthy to add to your Shop of Habits. Seed yourself something good. Something to make you want to wake up to live. Because from good, comes many more good things, and so we can presume that from good patterns, come many more good patterns, be mindful of your compounding results, they are dependent upon your patterns. And patterns, weave a free destiny, or a shackled prison to hold you away from the light of noon.

Free yourself from your bonds, free yourself from your Patterns, and Soar like the Eagle, the Eagle only soars because he Can and knows he can, don't expect yourself to soar when you don't even know you are Free, just beneath the patterns.

Just free.

Chapter 34
Hunger/Desire

"You want to be other than what you are – you can be if you know who god is….Here is the secret, this fabulous world of ours is nothing more than the appeasement of hunger. The whole vast world is for that purpose, to appease *your* hunger."

— Neville Goddard

A beast lies within us all, something that seeks and obtains more and more of whatever the interest is. Be it good or evil, fun or boring, destructive or creative. In the end the hole that it fills will *never ever* be filled, and the hunger? That my friend, is something that eats away at all precious pieces of one's life if it cannot be controlled and made into an ally by Will.

The hunger I speak of that causes disintegration is not one of food or sex but something far more hidden. This hunger is able to sour a person's day, claim happiness and hope or even cause death. Metaphorical death I speak of.

The Hunger I speak of is the hunger and base nature of the Illusory Mind, the Ego to fulfill and act just as the person views themself to be. So in turn many will feed a harmful habit or stimulate negative mental chatter for the simple reason that they subconsciously (at all times) believe that they are that person. They are the negative depressed and possibly even hopeless character - a shell of a person.

All dreams squeezed out and white washed. Renounce your Hunger for Pain. Renounce your Hunger to cause pain, but most importantly, renounce your current self to your Heart, and see the wonder you have for yourself. *For in the Heart lies wisdom, and that same instinctual wisdom whether apparent or not somehow created every single thing ever to be, including the ground you are standing on and it will continue to create, for life is the eternal appeasement of hunger.*

That which you desire for or hunger after, becomes. That which you allow yourself to get tripped up by, only exists because you brought it here in the first place with a past un"enlightened" hunger.

There are no Enlightened Hungers, for All already Is, it simply will continue becoming, and that *becoming* is the appeasement of the Universes hungers. You are the highest form of the Universe currently walking or to ever walk.

Your Soul is a Godspark and is a vast library of experience, your Mind - is an extension of all the Universe's Energies. A focuser and a tuner, just like a radio, your Body, is the Chariot and Vehicle that contains. For the great passenger that resides within, is the eternal ground of being in physical form - The *Self* - I Am.

Be in the state of your fulfilled desire, in the state of your appeased hunger, and you will have all that you wish, or ever could wish.

Chapter 35
Joyslayer

"Realize deeply that the present moment is all you have. Make the NOW the primary focus of your life."

— Eckhart Tolle

Distraction after distraction, leading on in life, yet feeling no traction? Maybe you have encountered Joyslayer, the killer of all change. Joyslayer's name is Procrastination, and it is not your friend.

Procrastination comes in a legion of forms, one or a few in the mind, one on the wrist, another in the pocket, and one that is a handheld computer called a cell phone, and that is the biggest one.

Nothing slays a person's Joy more than wanting to do something, not doing it, then looking back in regret. Regret is poison to the soul, free yourself of this burden by following through, be a doer, be a haver, it's a choice, not a condition.

If doing and having were Conditional, no new things would ever come to pass, and no new things would ever be had, for in Choice, is possibility, and in possibility is imagination.

Being a doer and a haver is a choice, because one cannot simply choose to abandon a previous lower state to adopt a higher state without first deciding and choosing to rise above your perceived conditions.

And basing possibilities on what conditions have come to pass is like saying you hate fishing because all you've ever fished in was a pond. To venture and fish in the big ocean, you have to choose to let go of the pond, but most importantly, you must let go of your hatred (or perspective) of "fishing" to then allow a new condition to be brought into being through choice. Condition reveals the flaw and weight that your desires place on your soul, sometimes the venom in your heart is from the immense effort you put in to accomplish some task or create some change, while still holding onto the previous state and perspective not allowing yourself to let go. And this death grip on the past condition, while holding the present desire in mind will create a split in yourself and energy.

The more weight a desire places on your Heart, usually shows the amount of attachment/identification to a current condition that you are tirelessly attempting to shift. Change starts within. Change starts with choice.

And choice can only happen if the mind can rise above condition and can be brave enough to imagine, and choose to change perspective to a more desire-affirming state of emotion and perspective.

This sounds blatantly stupid to the logical mind, and the logical mind looks retarded in the eyes of the Intuition and

Imagination, for Logic is the rigid aspect, the conditional, imagination and intuition, those are a choice,

Be in harmony within your mind and accept the flame of tempered reason and logic, but do not cut yourself off from Intuition and Imagination for as Einstein said, "I believe in intuition and inspiration. Imagination is more important than knowledge. For knowledge is limited, whereas imagination embraces the entire world, stimulating progress, giving birth to evolution.'

Chapter 36
Why Intuition?

"The only real valuable thing is intuition."

— Albert Einstein

Joan of Arc was told things about the future from what she called "God" within her conscious mind. To my curious and open perspective this means that she developed a connection between her conscious and subconscious minds, or her Illusory Self and Eternal Self, or Higher Self as some people call it. I like to just call it my Intuition. You see, if you are playing a game, and the game has to be played a certain way, wouldn't you like a map of where to step next to ensure you "win the game"?

Of course, but how does one get such a map? Well, first it isn't really a map, it's a Sign Post, it just guides you to the right direction. You have to concentrate your attention and intention on maintaining course, if you get lost, you can always find your way back into balance, but you will get lost. Do not forget to ask for help when you are lost, your Inner Self will always stretch out a hand.

This sign post I speak of isn't really one thing, it isn't really a cheat or a hack, but more just how your brain works. If you ask it a question, it must have an equal or greater reaction and thus, an answer must be formed for the question asked. Asking for help, or in this case asking a question, will bring the byproduct of a Sign Post.

This Sign Post, the answer to your question, is always determined by your question, so it's never about the answer, but the question.

Say you are lost within yourself and find it hard to organize yourself and life.

Try asking: If I had my life and self together how I could right now, how would I go forward? What things would I cut out for myself? What things would I add?

The really simple small steps take you to the end of the race. You'd be surprised to know that not that many people actually ask questions like that.

This type of success is not about what you can gain, but what you can become aware of to let go of.

All change starts with the realization of the desire to change, it's up to You, to follow the sign post The Guide Inside gifts to you. You can be the devil if you wish and lie to yourself about not Knowing, or you can "open the door to Heaven" by Embodying that which your gracious and helpful Intuition has prepared for you.

It all starts Now. And still will always end, Now.

Begin if you wish.

Continue as you have.

Most importantly, acknowledge that you have.

Chapter 37
The World's Best Boss

"Knowing yourself is the beginning of all wisdom."

— Aristotle

We all know those people that go on and on about how God told them this and God told them that. Well, what if that Source that the information is coming from is the Guide Inside? What if all those nudges, guidances, intuitions and suggestions are Divine Downstreamings of information? What if they are deceitful snares to lock you down into bad habits, and instead of Intuition it is self-hating comments? Taking you down a faucet in your mind.

What if all the characters and names you name for different information sources are your Self? If the Self is infinite, it must be able to take infinite forms; thus, when you receive information that is not a part of your normal train of thought you are getting tricklings of the liquid of pure or in some cases nasty information. This is a given, but most don't know that the place from which the information trickles down from is all the same place, just interpreted from different perspectives. Viewed from different lenses.

One of the most enthralling lenses is the lens of emotion. If you are in despair because of losing something or someone, the tricklings of information you receive will always be of a sorrowful nature. It is only when we realize "We cannot solve our problems with the same thinking we used when we created them" (Einstein), that we are able to change like a radio station ever so slowly from despair to anger, from anger to disappointment and from disappointment to acceptance or neutrality. Just as the radio stations change, so do our states, we are never static.

A well-groomed Boss of a person is a person that knows when to override the current station being played because of apparent self-sabotage and switch to a more productive and fruitful station, or in this case emotional state.

No one can Boss your mind except your Self. Your Self isn't your mind, your mind is your mind. When the thoughts and emotions of a certain radio station get too noisy to be able to "hear" the important stuff in life, like gratitude, we lose sight of reality and lose sight of ourselves and vision. Only you can Boss your mind because your mind doesn't boss you, unless you let it. The Illusory Mind's greatest dream and aspiration is to break you like a dog to follow its every command. Boss your mind, body and spirit back into harmony, only you can, it all starts with your Self.

If you let the thoughts (downstreamings of information) when in a certain state give you the impression that that is all there is or ever could be, your mind is bossing you; when you know confidently that you are no slave to the mind you will break free and fulfillment can be your nature.

You are the World's Best Boss, for your Self of course.

Chapter 38

The Father of Lies, Satan Himself

"Hell is empty and all the devils are here."

— William Shakespeare

Nothing enslaves more than the liar. The liar will tie strings so tightly around any situation that when the puppets actually dance and the people sing just like they wanted, they forget that they are lying to make it happen, and so the toughest and strongest cords wrap around the liar's mind until the marionette most dancing on strings is yourself. For this reason you can be your own Satan, your own Father of Lies.

The dirty atrocities of the world are usually collateral or direct damage from lies. Not pleasant white lies or beneficial encouragement but the filthy excuse for history and ethics that permeate all aspects of culture. People pride themselves on how well they can lie to themselves by getting in a group and spouting off at each other to see who can say the lie the best, in a way that most people would be receptive to. This kind of lie is that lie that will delude a whole nation to be silent during genocide right under their nose, this kind of lie, gets young "justice" seekers to condemn and reject the very people fighting for their freedom and accept the very people enlsaving those who the "justice" was to be wrought for.

Lies can be bliss. Ignorance can be bliss. Delusion can be bliss but the most dangerous and scary of blisses that exist out there in the far reaches of nothingness is Hypocrisy. Because a terrifying fact is that human nature is hypocrisy. That which one strikes down verbally and condemns is most definitely the correspondent thing that very person is also doing. You cannot dislike something in the outer world and not first find it as something you dislike within yourself.

You only see something as praiseworthy because it is something you admire, you only disgust at something if you first know of its filth from within your very soul. YOU, are everything you will ever judge. You can only judge something and reject it because it is rejected inside yourself first. A lazy person may hate and be spiteful towards those who work away tirelessly to feed their kids, for the only reason that they think they themselves should also be working and by virtue of hypocrisy don't want to admit they are wanting that and so project hate and spite and judgment to conceal and numb the wound of envy. Lie away to yourself as much as you wish, but when opportunities for condemnation and judgments arise, remember that within yourself also are those things. Accept that being an accepting person is truthful, powerful and wise.

For if you judge another by the thing you yourself would be guilty of, you are lying to yourself and smothering opportunity. Only the greatest self-deceit can bring about the inability to accept one's own hypocrisy. And thus most are possessed by the Father of Lies, Satan Himself, the state of unselfaware deceitful hypocrisy. Comfortable lies.

Chapter 39
The Blind Watcher

"Through our eyes, the universe is perceiving itself. Through our ears, the universe is listening to its harmonies. We are the witnesses through which the universe becomes conscious of its glory, of its magnificence."

— Alan W. Watts

Notice how with assumption one can go about any life in any place during any conditions and be blind to everything outside of what is assumed by that person. A showing of the news, some jump in joy, others sob and cry, the lens of assumption pulls one in and keeps them till it is turned into another. The good, the bad and the ugly just happen to rest on the shoulders of The Blind Watcher, for they stroll about life, casting the good as bad and the bad as good, when in reality neither was neither and nothing was understood. The language of The Blind Watcher is projection, for one projects out their assumption of what every little occurrence means subjectively to that person.

This world is a world of *placebos.* For those who do not know what a placebo effect is: It is a response or reaction that happens to a person about any possible thing in accordance with their *belief* of what is going to happen. Or in other words, whatever one assumes will come to pass, most likely will.

So project out your assumptions, and see what chaotic fish you bring back, for assumption doesn't discriminate. And the untrained assumption will plant seeds of poverty and scarcity, when the trained assumption knows better, knowing that God or the Universe or Allah will provide. Faith is the language of receiving, and gratitude is the down payment.

Assume that which you wish as already being present, leave the down payment of gratitude to insure that you will be receiving, and leave the rest of the exchange with Faith.

Lead on sightless, oh Blind Watcher, and cast down blessings as curses and welcome torment as sunshine, but do not curse the world or yourself for your projected assumptions, ye are in control of what you let go of or take on.

Let go of the security that paranoid assumptions provide, trust grows great trees from seeds planted, and doubt scorches the fields and makes planting temporarily impossible. Work through doubt, and see your assumptions change, add in faith and see your world change.

As within so without, as projected so received. Be the person seeing the impact of their own assumptions and not the sightless wanderer that continues their sleep. There are billions of Blind Watchers, not seeing with the trained assumption, only those who invest and give the down payment of gratitude and faith can reap the fruits of masterful assumption.

Luck is no such thing, only assumption, heaven or hell, enjoy playing the game.

Chapter 40
The Sun Will Come Up Tomorrow

"One more dance along the razor's edge finished. Almost dead yesterday, maybe dead tomorrow, but alive, gloriously alive, today."

— Robert Jordan

Ease the pressure of your mind, for the sun will come up tomorrow. You will live, you are living, you can still breathe, you have won. This is important to acknowledge, we don't give ourselves enough credit, yet still we lose ourselves in momentary mental chatter. Leave the jungle of complaints and go see the sky of clarity.

"I'm having a good day because my name is not in the obituary, how about that!" Mike Lyman- 2020 (What saddens me now as I write this, is my grandfather Lawrence Michael Lyman died September 9th, 2020, this quote is from summer time).

We go on and on, until we don't. We call that death, when death happens, we no longer can "do" anymore things. So does that mean life is all and only Doing? Is the universe a big Doing?

To what end? The gear keeps moving, the machine keeps building, but the parts are replaced, over and over and over again. What good is a machine? When the machine is automatic, lifeless? There is no flowing and moving and evolving without understanding the purpose of the machine? Is it a machine? No. Is a machine capable of Self-examination?

It seems this world is a byproduct, rather than the whole "Machine". Does this mean the physical world is like a car's AC drip that comes down, and as a byproduct of the whole, comes into being? (Meaning that the Universe is just a process of something much bigger that we can't see).

Chaos forged order? How could it be? If the machine's byproduct is the world, then how can Chaos create a machine? What complex chaos could birth the seeming incongruity of the physical world? If not the Order and blueprint of all things. The flower of Life, the Vesica Pisces, and all Sacred Geometries seem to be mandalas on spiritual tapestries and works, yet not as apparent in the physical. Yet when zoomed in on and observed "matter" functions as byproduct the Quantum, thus the Spiritual Tapestries and posters that bolster nice looking shapes and symbols as the "Universe" are seemingly accurate.

What machine, chaos or order can ordain all physical byproducts in its image? Its perfect image?

I'll give you a hint:

"Wisdom of Solomon 2:23: For **God created man to be** immortal, and made him to be an image of his own eternity. The righteous, because they are **made in the image of God,** can rest in the full hope of eternal life."

I am not a practicing religious person, but I Am the Image of God, just as you are.

To claim the crude matter that makes up our bodies is made in the image of God is absurd to the "intellectual" or "logically minded" individual, yet that individual knows nothing of their mother's Egg that was fertilized and makes up the shape of The Flower of Life, the blueprint.

If all matter is ordained in this way, and the chemical bonds of chemistry corresponde and form all bodies of mass in the image of God, what is the image of God?

If God is all things, it must be the cycle that moves the Sun, it must be the Sun that nurtures the Earth, the Earth that mothers the people and feeds them, the People that blossom and bloom and create, all physical things or doings, started first in the image of God-Infinity.

Which means it has No Image, it is infinite, thus cannot be conceived or symbolized or represented or even understood, for it is Void of Form. Form is its byproduct not its source.

In Quantum physics the Wave is eternal and utterly shapeless and formless, until converted into the Particle (form) through observation. Thus the "doing" of this world is the "doing" of the Particle, which came into being from the Wave. Vibration.

What does it mean to vibrate? It means to occelate. What does it mean to occelate? It means that "... that **energy** is always conserved, it **cannot be created or destroyed**." In essence, energy can be converted from one form into another." Third Law of Thermodynamics.

The "world" as we know it, is nothing more than a byproduct of our existence, the existence of the Wave, the existence of the One Consciousness, the existence of God, the unmanifest,

the formless infinity from which all was wrought. Consciousness, the "cause-substance" as Neville Goddard calls it.

Its eternal name is I Am.

You are it and so am I.

Chapter 41

Why do Humans have such a propensity towards Addiction?

"Every form of addiction is bad, no matter whether the narcotic be alcohol, morphine or idealism."

— C.G. Jung

Imagine a little child playing in the grass, grasping its precious toy, and all of a sudden some other slightly older child comes over and steals and destroys the child's precious toy. Now gone, the child's missing toy weighs in on the child's heart making it cry. A worried mother soothes the child's tears and asks it why it was crying? It responds "I want my toy back". Now having the burden of having to explain to the child that the toy no longer exists, the mother avoids telling them they can't have what they once did, the innocent good-intentioned mother will either grab another toy for the child, or if they are the gift type, will go to the store and pick out a new toy for the child to replace what they had lost.

That is the problem with addiction. The thing we all "lost" was ourselves, our connection, not our human selves, but our Spiritual Self, the Soul if you wish.

Imagine running around a planet and expecting to be able to replace something or find it, but you can't quite put your finger on what you have lost, or what you want to find, that is the main cause for addiction, we lack recollection of Ourselves. Of the majesty of the Soul.

Only to find fleeting moments of gratification that only soothe the physical senses, you are left utterly empty and void in the spiritual regard. How can you do anything that feels good, if the things that are to feel good are but half things, half fillers, half stimulators. Even experience in the outer world when experienced through a dead perspective or numb place of mind seems to be the thing sought for, as if some small piece is missing and with that piece, all of your problems or hungers will go away.

That "piece" is the void in people's hearts, the void and emptiness of a person who strives for more, but doesn't know what the more is, a person not content with their millions and wants true connection, real feeling, real life, real aliveness.

Where can this "piece" be found? How can this "piece" be gotten? How can we claim this birthright? What impossible task must we complete to find this invisible "piece"? Where must we seek, what must we do, how will we achieve?

These are all logical questions in the sense that they are directed to find a solution. But the questions are flawed, you see. They are directed as if the "piece" can be found somewhere "out there". That in some impossible way the "piece" or toy we had taken from us, is in some way in the physical world, in the byproduct, in the effect of the cause.

We can search and search and sate and hunger more and find and lose and gain and surrender and rise and fall, but we will always be void and empty until *we let go*.

You can only "create" a new foundation if the rubble of the previous structure is cleared. You have to let go. It isn't about what we can "add" to ourselves or gain but rather what we let go of to create space for.

See the "piece" was never lost ever and can never be lost, it is You, inner you, your soul, your being, your higher self or your higher power, whatever you call it, IT IS YOU.

If you place some outer world thing on a pedestal as the thing that will redeem you or complete you, you, my friend, are in for self-created damnation and eternal searching. How can you search when there is nothing there? Nothing to search for.

That's exactly it - There is Nothing to search for. The "piece" is Nothing. The state of letting go of the illusion of physical salvation, the sense of completion from some "thing". Completion already is, creation already happened, you already are, I still Am.

You cannot gain anything you do not already have, for "having" as we humans see it, is a state of material possession, but physical having is just the byproduct, not the cause. It's the effect not the source.

The Nothingness I spoke of, the "piece" we lost yet never lost, is Consciousness, consciousness aware of itself, what you were looking for was Presence, awareness of the infinite, the shedding of "form" and the realization of the immortal void, the eternal nothingness, the omnipresent consciousness that is you.

Now this sounds like a bunch of mumbo-jumbo, because it is, because I am attempting to put something indescribable into words for minds to attempt to digest, but the "finding" of the missing piece isn't an outside job, but rather an inner one, one of Mind or Heart, one Self not other, one of Inner Reality, one of dissolution, dissolving and melting all that is known, to courageously surrender into nothingness and let go of your belief system, let go of your thoughts, let go of all processes and just be.

Some call it meditation, or prayer or chanting or any other way you do it, it can even be fishing. A wink to my Father. (He calls Fishing his meditation.)

Some call it being in the present moment, be here now. Some call it mindfulness, be aware of your thoughts and emotions so you don't become them. Some call it Nirvana or Satori, others call it Enlightenment. It is simply the "lighting" up of your awareness of the Infinite and releasing yourself from the endless chase of completion. It's believing and knowing and experiencing Perfection Now.

(There have been some months of transformation in between now and when I wrote the above words, since then, my grandfather has passed, I've started a business and gotten a second job, I have been busy, but I have found that in this time of character development my connection to the Guide has gotten better.)

Chapter 42
Sundrops

"Most humans were not malicious, only drastically misguided and desperate in their loneliness. They learned at some point that there was an eccentric core to their personality and that it was possible no one else shared their own brand of eccentricity. They put up screens around that core to shield from embarrassment and shame. For all the pompous forms in which writers and musicians have described it, love was surely that moment when the screens might come down in front of another human, if only for a moment, and freely give them a long, unfettered look into the true middle where the fear and anguish lives."

— Exurb1a[sic] - (The Fifth Science)

"Hope is like a flicker of a flame dancing in my heart. When my heart closes, the flame of hope dies along with it, but the heart can always be reopened" Your's truly.

Gem after gem, achievement after achievement, nod after nod, but still never enough to stop the doubtful insecure mind.

It cannot be stopped, for like a leech it seeks to harvest the blood and being of all the substance of You. That's right your own mind is a parasite sometimes that when not kept in check, feeds on your regrets and griefs to sate it's lonely sense of salvation, a "I told you so" to the heart. See, when the parasite is active, its salvation is your suffering, for in your suffering you do not change, and in not changing you sustain your parasitic mind.

This may come as a shock to some: "I don't have parasites in my mind?!", "Did he say my brain is a parasite?", "Is he trying to say we humans are the parasites?"

No, none of this. I am simply stating the fact that if one is to look at their own self-sabotage and fear, and truly look at it, one will come to the conclusion eventually that all hopes and dreams , if NOT accomplished or sought after, will inherently feed off of you and your insecurities will thrive and inno-cently succor you to give in, and by giving in, you give up, and in giving up, you die along with your dreams, never to see the light of day above the shifting mass of shadow you've so keenly cowered away from facing-yourself.

The sun doesn't illuminate the mind of a man or woman that does not illuminate themselves to their shadow, the shadow and deeper self are but Sundrops at the end of labyrinth and cave of pains and sorrows, only to be held by those with the searing power of self-forgiveness, for only the self-forgiving person my see themselves, not as their shadow, but as they are.

We struggle to catch these Sundrops, whether in form of hope or intuition, or encouragement and happiness, but we cannot grasp the depth of the Blazing Pearl we grasp when our mind is stuck as a parasite, harvesting the bad of all we experience, feeding, tasting and drinking in all the melancholy and longing vibrations (emotions), stifling the potential of the blazing pearl of hope or desire, to only shred it of any validity and to self-condemn and self-shame for thinking that some possibility out there (in the world) or even in here (in your mind) could possibly be purifying enough to awaken us from the parasite state, feeding off of our own sorrows, to smack us awake to reality and let us see ourselves for once.

The purpose of this book is to: illuminate the shadow of your Self so that you see the Guide beneath the shadow, always happy to provide, only waiting for your command or seeking.

Chapter 43
We Want, but hate ourselves for Wanting

"A child can teach an adult three things: to be happy for no reason, to always be busy with something, and to know how to demand with all his might that which he desires."

— Paulo Coelho

Freedom and peace and prosperous feelings are at a finger's distance from you, all you must do is love yourself.

If you ask the average Joe, "Hey, do you love yourself" some will say yes, some will nod because they'll think it's what you want to hear, but few, truly few, will question and realize the truth, no, no they don't love themselves. And that is the truth of our planet, many love themselves, many lie to themselves, but even more don't know that you can love yourself or should.

We are lost, seeking intimacy in a sea of self-hate, how does one go forward purified from the bile of self-hatred? Forgiveness, to fully let go, to abandon.

What happens to a snake when it sheds its skin? Does it die? Does it change form? Does it let go of a part of itself?

Go forward as the snake shedding its skin of self-loathing, for only your skin is yours, and all things must die to be reborn.

To forgive and forget, to let go of and abandon, and let be. There seems to be a longing for completion or closure in our hearts, even for the smallest things, I think that's because we cannot let go.

Just like the bliss and high of novelty or that new thing or experience or show or person, once it fades and has reached its peak and fallen, what then? Why does life live when we start, yet feel like it dies when we end something? Bittersweet a small death, a small letting go of, what could this be?

Do I seek salvation in the things I do? No, but I wish they could last forever. Or to be able to feel how you did the first time you did something again, after having done it thousands of times.

If we're always connecting, but never letting go, we die more and more, until we let go. But in letting go, we create room for more connecting and inevitably revive. I speak figuratively of life and death, more as *life* as the will to thrive and death as the desire to stagnate (when someone asks how you are doing and you say "Just living" because you are doing just that, just existing, not doing what you want).

Forgiving is letting go. If I were Hitler, all but God would say I should hold onto my sins for the price of the lives I'd taken, yet far worse men have lived than Hitler and somehow there isn't a limiter to evil. Evil is evil, it's just that, pain. Those pained who cannot let go of the pain, and so to not deal with the pain of facing the pain, one will cause all around them the same pain they are enslaved by. This is where "misery likes company" comes from, and so to the miserable many, who cannot forgive the world and cannot forgive themselves, ask your Self this:

What possible atrocity could I commit that God would not forgive me for?

None, for even God is capable of evil. Evil, good, bad, decent, amazing, horrible, the individual, everything, all of the universe has come to this here point and we judge ourselves for what we know not we do, and cast down our ignorant arrogance as Evil and believe truly that we are sinned and terrible and parasites, but this is false. We simply have forgotten to let go, let go of hate, let go of fear, let go of shame, let go of guilt, let go of grief, let go of lies, let go of envy, let go of ignorance so we can stop polluting the mind of all with our arrogance. We are not evil, or good. Evil does not exist, because everything is inherently meaningless, but pain does exist and pain is what causes atrocities.

Do what God would do for you and forgive yourself, you need not bear the shames of all ignorance, all you must do is hold the flame of truth and pierce through your own self-deception and see, that you too, can love yourself and forgive yourself, for even God would, unless you are that arrogant to think there was no one worse than you before, you prideful fool.

Chapter 44
A Vial of Vile Poison

"I fear that on my last day, on my deathbed, that is when the meaning of things will enter the room and kiss my forehead and whisper into my ear what it was I should have done with my life, and how I should've conducted myself. Hell isn't a fire pit but a museum of regrets."

— Exurb1a[sic] - (The Fifth Science)

You want to leave, you don't want to be seen, you don't want to look into their eyes, or at your own, you want to fly free in the abyss of your own shame and forget the future so you have a reason to always be sad, loathing the presence of your own mind, to be shattered not self-accepting - drowning in the cuts of judgment from your mind only to realize, I don't accept myself, and this is the reason your shame is flaying you, you must accept yourself.

A vile poison is one that kills slowly. Everyone knows a quick death is a merciful death, but for vile poisons? Only the excruciating corrosion of your mind and heart as the poison crushes your soul will convince you that poison is not what you want. Shame is the long winded poison, the poison that keeps pace with you, like a shadow, smiles and taunts your every action, waiting to strike again with another "I told you so!"

Shame is the mind killing its creations and stopping action for the sake of wanting to beat itself to a pulp. Do you want to squeeze your mind and ring it out and see what lies of shame fall out? See how you would see if you accepted yourself, and see how different it is to how you do now.

To cure patients of a poison that works slowly, one must come up with a permanent cure. Since the ailment is shame and shame is dependent on the past, this cure must have to do with the past. Maybe it has to do with how the patient sees themselves in regard to their past? What role they played or what they believe they deserve. Guilt and shame in the heart will corrupt all new blessings leaving one option as reasonable: face it.

Chapter 45
Acceptance, True Acceptance

"And that is, you see, the most difficult thing to do, to accept oneself completely. Because the moment you can do that, you have in effect done psychologically what is the equivalent of saying in philosophical or theological terms, you, as you are now, are the Buddha...that's unbelievable. Because we are always trying to get away from ourselves as we are now, in one fashion or another, and we will only stop doing that through a series of experiments in which we try resolutely to get away from ourselves as we are, so that is the middle way."

— Alan Watts

What does it mean to accept oneself fully? To me it is to be nothingness. Does the self-defined state you are in encapsulate your entire being? No, it is an emotion or state of mind, that means my "full self" is not the state I am in or the mental state I am in, it is an all encompassing stillness that pierces the temporary definitions we give ourselves. Some call it presence or awareness or consciousness, these all work, but it is far subtler than a word, or really anything we can fathom. We have to experience it to know it, or rather to remember it.

How do we experience it? The Guide Inside, the still and silent nothingness in the void of our minds is experienced by Meditation, by breathing techniques, for some with psyche-delics or infinite different ways. To know it and experience it is different than hearing about it, one must dive into their soul to get this kinda show. Widen your horizons; you haven't seen anything yet.

Chapter 46
God Of Perception

"As you sow in your subconscious mind, so shall you reap in your body and environment."

— Joseph Murphy

Imagine for a moment an all-seeing/experiencing God. Every fall of lightning, drop of water and breath is seen, felt, and experienced. It is without difficulty that the God of Perception takes note of every little fine detail of what happens in front and around and above and below and within and without and as self and as other as micro and macro as God and Creation.

Now that little tidbit is pretty much what your Subconscious is, roughly speaking of course. How, you may ask? Well, how is simple, there are about 50 bits of information processed by your Conscious Mind and 11 Million bits processed by your Unconscious Mind aka your Subconscious or the "Guide Inside" whatever the fuck you want to call it.

Your heart beats thousands and thousands of times a day without you knowing how to beat your own heart. You don't need to "know" how to move a body part, you get the idea and act on it and it happens, there is no in between. Now you may say well you learned how to do it as a baby, well I say this: How do you automatically know how to keep your thoughts going on and on and on and on. You don't know, it just happens. See its unconscious, automatic, autopilot. How do you drive somewhere when zoned out and not crash, ah autopilot. Wonderful, that aside, what do you think happens when you become conscious while in the unconscious? You guessed it, you have a lucid dream, just kidding I know you didn't guess that, or maybe you did. See, waking up while still dreaming is a bizarre experience, it shows the fluidity of what we call reality.

I once stood on a foreign beach wiggling my toes in the sand with small flat waves and a reflecting sea, with a beautiful towering spire on a mountain in the distance, and I realized "Oh shit, I'm dreaming!' The first thing I did was calm myself and imagine I was breathing to relax. See, too much of any emotion is unstabilizing to dreams and can make you wake up. Be cool, be serene and tranquil, but most impor- tantly be intentional and single minded. With a wholehearted focus and an uttering of the words "I demand Clarity" outloud, my dream stabilized and I saw the beach and still felt the nice sand in between my toes, but I looked down and got worried, startled really.

I didn't have a body, I was completely see-through with no part of me visible. But, I did feel like I was in a full physical and normal body, while feeling like everything around me I could perceive was an extension of my body. I decided I wanted a body. So I intended for my body to come back. I then saw bones knitting and flesh weaving up and blood and tendons and flesh and everything knitting and spiraling up. And whoosh! I was in my normal body! I then decided I wanted to take advantage of the time in my Unconscious and learn to fly. I decided to float, I said, "Float". My body sprung up in the air two feet. It was disconcerting because I felt like I was gonna roll or or shift my weight wrong and fall face first.

After what I would say was about 30 seconds I finally was able to fly and I decided to check out the aforementioned Tower in the distance and I rushed towards it like a comet with my hair blowing wild and mouth catching the cool breeze.

Chapter 47
Time Flies When You're Having Fun

"Life lives on life. This is the sense of the symbol of the Ouroboros, the serpent biting its tail. Everything that lives lives on the death of something else. Your own body will be food for something else. Anyone who denies this, anyone who holds back, is out of order. Death is an act of giving."

— Joseph Campbell

Four months have passed since my last entry. This is a good thing. I notice that time gets stagnant sometimes and then after the little knot in the rope gets untied, much, much time passes. Like a slide down a hill, at first your body is stuck on the entry, then after scooting forward and freeing yourself, all of a sudden you start sliding and can't stop and before you know it you're at the bottom of the hill.

The dread of the 24- hour day can be how finite it is, only 78 twenty minute periods, like 78 episodes of a show, and boom you're up again. Hours and minutes and weeks and months are finite because they are representations of allotments of time, symbols. You don't know how long an hour is when you experience an hour because it flows according to your emotional state. An hour can be a moment, or an hour can be eternity. The determining factor is you, *You* you.

Is it bad for hours to fly by if you are in an inspired, creative state, fully energized by the Guide Inside to make or create or seek or find something, and time, just like in a race, warps around you until your task is completed? No, this is how we use time to our advantage. Time will collapse, no matter what and weeks will pass like hours. The question is: can you make the minutes in the hour-long weeks be as productive as possible, while maintaining the Will for Discipline and the will to care to care? Absolutely you can.

How do you do it? You have to create space, block out 5 or 10 minutes and just sit and do nothing with your mind and body, N-O-T-H-I-N-G at all, just breathe and observe all the random thoughts from minutes to hours to weeks ago pop up and see how much clutter there is. How do you clean the clutter of the mind? Be still, while seeing the torment of all your thoughts and don't engage any thoughts more than any others for they are all just thoughts.

This space or gap between the automatic flow of the river of thought, gives space for new flow, new currents, new waves and new streams. But how can there be a new stream, if there is no new current? And how can the new current added not just get swept up by more dominant streams of thought and just get engulfed, absorbed, eaten and eventually forgotten as just another current in the distracting river of endless thoughts: space, you need to create space.

What is space? Emptiness, not in the traditional glass half empty sense, but rather the emptiness of the whole glass or cup, that contains the water. As the amazing Bruce Lee said

"You must be shapeless, formless, like water. When you pour water in a cup, it becomes the cup. When you pour water in a bottle, it becomes the bottle. When you pour water in a teapot, it becomes a teapot. Water can drip and it can crash. Become like water, my friend."

If you have no space for awareness, how do you expect you'll ever come to your senses about what needs to change? You won't, you'll just exist thinking you're living until you die, never having lived, only having existed, and then you will die.

Meditation is a nasty word for most people, the thought of emptying one's mind is ever more disturbing once you try it a few times and realize just how hard it is. Let me tell you a secret: it isn't about emptying your mind, it's about disengaging it, unattaching yourself from each thought.

What happens when you're at a party or event with loud noises in the background or many people talking and you focus on one person in front of you, or rather what they are saying? You can tune out the background noise and narrow in on the object of focus.

Now say you were able to do that and tune out your background thoughts while grasping the space in which they happen, almost like being formless and realizing anytime anything comes to captivate you to focus on form, you stop thinking about the object and start feeling the energy or space, giving thoughts a quality like pucks sliding on ice, they don't stay in one place, they flow.

What would happen? You would see that events are fluid like thoughts and are waiting to spring into motion, but the automatic train of thought which guides the action is impeded by the current flow or stagnation of energy. How do you do something different, if every time you do something, you still have the same perspective about what you're doing, smothering like oil on water, tainting and sabotaging any and all results with the unsavory flavor of self-judgment. You have to create space, space for mind, space for thought, space for perspective and space for energy, new energy, new flow, new current, new motion.

"All men's miseries derive from not being able to sit in a quiet room alone." -Blaise Pascal

You get the picture.

Chapter 48
Anamnesis

"I searched myself in the pearls of words, shining in the midnight, I found only the infinite Anamnesis with a Dead-eye"

— Unknown

Roughly meaning "loss of forgetfulness" in Greek, is a word I much like. It strangely is synonymous to me with Enlightenment, or Nirvana (to be Blown Out). It points to a simple fact: humans spend more time in the dream of forgetfulness than in consciousness.

To change brainwave states or to enter one's subconscious mind is an experience much like what I was describing in the above statement. For in entering an Alpha or Theta brainwave state your day-to-day mind or monkey mind has a change in focus, instead of endless continuous thought, bouncing from one concept or complaint or hope or dream to the next and the next and the next, it goes into passive, observer mode.

Providing the mind with a sense of ease and detachment. Conceptually this is great, but experientially this is about the worst concept possible to explain. But here we go, I will do my best:

Imagine a bobber (the floaty thingy on a fishing line that stays floating naturally) Now imagine that every time the bobber goes underwater, because it can float, it will rise up back to the surface no matter what. Now, what would happen if the bobber tried to stay under? Eventually it would have to come back to the surface because that's its natural motion. You wouldn't expect it to do something unexplainable, it just does what it always does. Great! That aside, well, I'd like to introduce you to your Mind or at least what you call your Mind, it's more like your Attention. Now imagine that just like the bobber's natural motion, which is to rise to the surface, the Mind's natural motion is to "rise to the surface", with this we can get a rough idea of how the Mind works. Imagine that the surface is your day-to-day mind; the problems you're creating solutions for, the trains of thought you're having, the complaints, lusts, hopes and dreams, and just about anything and everything in the Conscious Mind. Great, so since the Mind <u>automatically</u> "rises to the surface" just like the bobber, the rest of the Ocean (The Subconscious Mind/The Guide Inside) is left doing its thing in the background; running your heart, bringing oxygen and blood around, digesting, and regulating your hormones and such, background processes, unconscious things, so that all the bobber really experiences is the Surface, because its natural motion is to float. As you well know, the ocean is massive, and a bobber, well you know it's not so massive, in fact compared to the whole of the ocean, it's just a sandgrain, an itty bitty miniscule tiny almost invisible piece to the whole of the ocean, well, that's the difference between the Conscious Mind and the Subconscious Mind. One is a Behemoth, another is a Fly, yet for some reason, us humans think the Fly has all the power, when the

Behemoth is sleeping awaiting command. Just like the Bobber will touch many parts of the surface of the Ocean, but never, ever see the vastness of its depths, you too are on the surface of the great ocean of God, which is You, and You, too, are but a fly gazing into Infinity, hoping to understand, or better yet, Know. This is a great work of understanding, to contemplate the vastness of one's Unconscious Self in comparison to one's Conscious Self, it yields only the best of results, for in this quest, one may very well answer the greatest question of all time: Who Am I? And I do not wish to spoil the answer for you so I'll leave you a clue: I Am that I Am. Back to the metaphor - Now imagine what could happen if instead of having Bobber on the fishing line, you put a Weight on instead, to help the bait sink to the bottom. Well instead of naturally floating up back to the surface, the Weight will bring the line all the way down to the bottom of the Ocean, where all the creepy crawlies and delicious yummies are. And just like that, you catch a fish of the likes that you've never seen, because it doesn't frequent the parts of the Ocean close to the surface, like the iceberg peeking its head out of the water, but maintaining its body of mass underwater. So what's the "Weight" you could use to enmesh your Conscious Mind and Subconscious Mind? In a sense, the weight is to become Conscious in the Unconscious, well it's called Meditation, or Sleep or Resting, or doing just about anything that enables you to <u>Feel</u> instead of <u>Think.</u> Don't worry, the thoughts you think won't disappear if you stop thinking them, in fact you can't "stop" thinking them, all you can do is stop "engaging" them, or stop attaching to them as they present themselves in your Mind. Ever notice how when you hang over a cliff or look over an edge, sometimes you imagine what it would be like to jump or to fall, not for the sake of dying or killing yourself, just for the curiosity of what it would be like to fall? People call that the 'Call of the Void" and it is well docu-

mented, but what it shows is a perfect example of how thoughts are always there, we just become aware of them. Two perfectly similar people could be standing next to each other looking out from on top of a mountain and one will feel the thing called the "Call of the Void" while the other contemplates 2 weeks from now and what they will have to do for errands. The only difference is the fact that one thought is engaged vs another, it's entirely possible for the opposite person to think the other thought but the thought they are currently engaging is overpowering their attention. Now imagine that all possible thoughts you could have, good, bad, ugly, despicable, holy, sanctified or empathetic all exist Now. Ready to be engaged, the barrier between all thoughts is simply the fact that the Conscious Mind can only focus on a small amount of things at once, so it pushes the unnecessary to the back of the mind to leave room for choice. Now you may be wondering, how does the room for choice created by the limitation of the Conscious Mind's processing power lead to the example experience of 1. 'The Call to the Void' or 2. Worrying about errands in the future, when those are just 2 potential thoughts among millions of other possible thoughts? Emotion, your state, how you feel. "The Call to the Void" isn't an evil temptation or bad experience, it is just one of many different contrasting experiences, it is the experiencer or talker who deems it bad, but to the person <u>feeling</u> it in the moment, it is most likely just childlike curiosity. Now the other person, whose diligently worrying about two weeks ahead has convinced himself that he is justified in his worry because it "feels productive" and it may very well be, in regard to getting the gears of thought to turn but what it shows is that based on his <u>emotional state</u> the thoughts he or she is having or <u>engaging</u> in are different from other possible thoughts. There is no right thought or wrong thought, only different thoughts, from a Psychological perspective (which *really means from a perspective of agreed principles of how the mind works dependent upon cultural or systemic biases based on current Theories) the "Call to the Void" thought may be labeled as unhealthy or perhaps worrisome, when in reality it is just the expression of one potential outcome, in the midst of infinite potential outcomes. Why does any of this matter or even contribute to the Bobber in the Ocean analogy? It shows that the <u>Ocean</u> (Unconscious Self) <u>does not discriminate between good or evil, bad or better, one thought or another, **it just is**</u>. And just like ripples eventually settle down back into the flow of the ocean, so do thoughts ripple and relax through the mind, never being absolute or permanent, but instead being drops and ripples in an Ocean. So if the thoughts are always there ready to be engaged, then does that mean the Thought is not the Cause, but rather the Effect? Does that mean that the thought is the Symptom and not the Root Cause? To me, yes. But I know not all there is to know, what I do know is this: The emotional state you are in is like a wave, pushing the water in front of it along with it, causing forward motion. Notice that the Wave does not care what kind of Momentum it has, it just keeps moving forward. The tsunami does not think "I am killing people, I must stop moving forward" it thinks "I am an inevitable effect, what I do is not good or bad, but just a result of what already happened, and thus I move forward." Now to the people, the tsunami is a wrecker, destroyer or perhaps a vengeful god, but to the Self, it is another part of itself. And so our emotions are like waves that move thoughts forward relentlessly and purposefully, not caring that the thoughts may be damaging or worsening the emotional state, just as the tsunami may lead to worse disasters or flooding. Now what happens when one chooses to "create" a wave, or guide the stream of the flow consciously? It is no longer the tsunami who destroys, but rather the wave that can be surfed upon and enjoyed. This* *is all metaphoric jibber jabber and I want to get back to the point: <u>You are the Ocean, you forget that you are the Ocean, by mistaking yourself as the Bobber, that always floats on the surface, ever forgetful to the depths of its own Self, moved by the waves the Self itself creates and lost to the Thoughts that stream in continually, temporarily castrating itself from itself to find and know itself again. Or rather Remember itself.</u> That is what Anamnesis means: loss of forgetfulness. Or in Ocean terms: The Bobber stops being a bobber and puts on the Weight, to sink to the depths of the Ocean to Remember that the Ocean is massive and all-encompassing and ANY fish you catch is just another part of the Whole of the Ocean. What good is this information? If You or your Higher Self or The Guide Inside or the Self or Source or God or your Inner Being or your Subconscious/Unconscious Self is the Whole of the Ocean, including all possible catchable fish (thoughts), then why not fish for the best fish? And not the nasty bottom feeders? If you're the Whole Ocean, and any and all fish (thoughts) that swim inside the Ocean are prepared and ready to be engaged (caught), then what holds you back from choosing to fish in different parts of the Ocean you usually don't? Ignorance, or amnesia if you wanna call it that. <u>The Bobber when its gasps for fresh air as it breaks out of the Ocean and back to the Surface isn't in the least bit concerned with the contents of the Ocean, it just wants to breathe</u> and thus <u>automatically</u> forgets the beauty of the Whole of the Ocean instead chooses to engage fully with whatever fish it sees itself capable of catching or in direct words: The attention when it exits the Unconscious Mind and enters back into the Conscious, can do nothing but forget the Entirety of the Infinite Ocean it just emerged from, if not, it would be overwhelmed. This is a good thing, for it leaves room for growth, for if the fisherman knew that it had already caught every single possible fish, from every time period ever, in every way* *possible, there wouldn't be much fun in fishing anymore. And whatever adventures would be had would become chores instead of adventures. For this reason we have momentary Amnesia when we change brainwave states (or changes the level that the Weight or Bobber is at) so that if we go from Active (Beta) to Receptive (Alpha or Theta) the experience of Mind is different and more Subconscious (less stream of consciousness types of thoughts and more "block of thought" or "download" or just "feeling" a "knowing" types of thought). And thus when we return to the surface after fishing, it's pretty difficult to wonder what it's like underwater when we have the fish in our hands.*

That was my attempt to explain how we have amnesia as a trigger to show when we go from Unconscious to Conscious, and it serves as the barrier between Lower Self and Higher Self, Creation and Creator, Self and God, I and All. And if we can master this <u>feeling awareness</u> from "ah I justed zoned out" to "oh I was just in my Subconscious" we can harness the Behemoth or Tsunami or the Ocean of the Universe Itself, instead of changing the world as the Fly, and consciously engage the Subconscious to do our bidding so that we too, become Co-Creator and not Co-Created.

Chapter 49
How In The F**k Do We Do That?

"If you try to change it, you will ruin it. Try to hold it, and you will lose it."

— Lao Tzu (Tao Te Ching)

Well we need some sort of gauge. Something to "measure" what state of mind we are in. Normally I would reiterate the "Astonishing Power of Emotions" As Abraham Hicks says but all that is is an explanation of the simple fact that: when you <u>feel good</u>, you are thinking and acting in accordance with your desire fulfilled, when you <u>feel bad</u>, you are thinking and acting opposite to what you would be doing if your desire was being fulfilled. But that is key in Manifestation of all sorts, but we are not talking about manifesting here.

Here we are talking about 'how to consciously change brain-wave states' to access more of our 'Guide Inside' or 'Subconscious Mind' or neurologically speaking: accessing our Right-Brain.

To not overwhelm you with explanations and theories I will keep it simple:

(I realize after writing this part that I failed to keep my promise and not give explanations and theories, but they are the training wheels for your Consciousness Bike. Bear with me.)

1. The types of thoughts you are having Now, perfectly reflect which level of Mind you are at.

   - For example: If you are having normal day to day linear thoughts, thinking about your To-Do list or errands or observation type thoughts, or just pondering or thinking normally about things.

(This is Beta or Conscious Mind)

2. The types of thoughts where you are feeling or rather thinking and feeling hopes, dreams or expectations and are still 'active" but more "daydream" type thoughts with a more active imagination

   - For example: you're sitting on the bus waiting for the ride to be over, looking out the window, just going with the flow of whatever enters your mind, not aiming in any specific direction but more so just observing what is there. Often this state is entered while listening to someone speak, or watching TV or reading a book, it is a passive, receptive state of mind.

(This is Alpha or Conscious while Semi-Subconscious)

3. Is when you Consciously relax the mind and body and choose to open your focus, not thinking about day to day things, more so just being in the Now, being present to the moment.

- For example: You want a small nap, you lay on your bed after a long gym workout or day of work and just sink into the soft cushion, letting go of all stress and giving the mind a break. Often is surrendered into or done consciously through meditation or breathing exercises. Also is the Dream state where REM sleep occurs (Rapid Eye Movement and increased brain activity in both Hemispheres of the brain to create Hemi Sync effect). Often experienced while conscious as a slight oceanic floating body sensation or lightness of body, where relaxation is so strong that it is bordering on sleep paralysis.

(This is Theta or Conscious in the Subconscious)

P.S To become Conscious while fully in the Subconscious takes practice or Lucid Dreams, often also occurring during deeper Meditations.

4. The blackout point moments before sleep ensues, similar to passing out or losing consciousness, often experienced as 'Coma Sleep'.

- For example: You are incredibly tired and watching a movie, you start falling asleep, over and over, but you are catching yourself every time and waking back up. Just to get even more tired to the point that you do fall asleep, but right before you fall asleep you have momentary Consciousness in the Subconscious experienced as a very rapid dream and then BOOM nothing, just blackness, void. The rapid onslaught of visuals or dreams is the progression from level 2 to 3 and then when the black out hits it is level 4. This level is the most restorative for the body, because all external focus is stopped and the mind is fully 'asleep'.

(This is Delta or Pure Subconscious)

P.S Due to the "blackout point" somewhere in between Theta (level 3) and Delta (Level 4) this is the best state to aim for to interact in the Subconscious because during the moment of "falling asleep" (Going into Delta or level 4) we have a neurotransmitter called Glutamate release and our perception of time gets funky; one moment may seem to be an hours worth of time or 3 hours may seem to be one moment. Due to this amazing biological technology we have the ability to CHOOSE to become Conscious while in the Subconscious by purposefully going with a sleepy feeling and maintaining conscious awareness of the change in mental states that proceeds the blackout into unconsciousness or Delta (level 4).

Note that Thomas Edison and many other famous characters in history have said that "the state bordering on sleep is where ideas are best birthed" and to utilize it, Mr. Edison would hold magnets in his hands while resting in a chair with his hands over bowls so that when he would fall asleep or go into Delta, he would drop the magnets into the bowl and the clang would wake him back up. Now if you repeat this after being awoken, you will enter the "bordering on sleep" state much quicker because you are already drowsy, in this state, ideas can be fished for, autosuggestions may be said with amazing results due to the fact you are saying them to the Subconscious itself or the Ocean as I previously called it instead of saying them while only in the state of the Bobber or Conscious Mind and not having results. It can also be used for rehabilitation and trauma release because of the more observer mode of mind that is active during this state (less attachment to the emotions of the trauma).

Chapter 50
Once More, How The F**k Do We Do That?

"The Formless Way-

We look at it, and do not see it; it is invisible.

We listen to it, and do not hear it; it is inaudible.

We touch it, and do not feel it; it is intangible.

These three elude our inquiries, and hence merge into one.

Not by its rising, is it bright,

nor by its sinking, is it dark.

Infinite and eternal, it cannot be defined.

It returns to nothingness.

This is the form of the formless, being in non-being.

It is nebulous and elusive.

Meet it, and you do not see its beginning.

Follow it, and you do not see its end.

Stay with the ancient Way

in order to master what is present.

Knowing the primeval beginning is the essence of the Way."

— Lao Tzu

Here is an exercise you can experiment with to see the various layers of Mind you have. The goal of the exercise isn't to produce a certain change in your mind or psychology or any sort of change at all. The goal is to show the natural processes your mind goes through when you sleep or meditate or choose to relax. And by watching the effects of your difference in focus you too can learn how to determine when you are in a Subconscious state or as I like to call it "union with the Guide Inside". So that you can consciously, at will, lower your brainwave state to enable you to think bigger or feel more, or intuit more, and really just about anything you can imagine can happen when you learn to become Conscious while in the Subconscious. It's where true magic happens and possibilities never thought of arise, it is the body of all potential and knowing, and from this state of Consciousness arose all creations of Man, and will ever arise more creations, for ever and ever and ever and ever. Because that's what You are, the You you that is eternal and is a 'Soul', all you are is Infinity. And this is one amazing way for you to experience that Infinity:

Step 1. **Relax**. Sit, lie down, or get comfortable in any way that you like. Just make sure you're able to close your eyes and be able to rest.

Step 2. **Breathe**. Breathe, breathe, breathe, and just keep breathing.

Step 3. **Notice**. As you breathe you WILL get distracted and that's okay! The key is paying attention to your change in focus and to notice when you get distracted that you are distracted.

(When you get distracted it's a sign of what level of mind you are at. The moment you notice distracting thoughts that pop out of nowhere, you know you starting to descend into the Subconscious, because when thoughts pop out of nowhere, its like you seeing the background processes of a computer, it's not that they are new processes, they were there the whole time, you just relaxed your focus enough by breathing that the normal processes that take your attention aren't taking your attention any more so now the background processes come to the surface) .

Step 4. **Ease** and **Slide**. Just like oil layered on water, our thoughts are like a film over our mind, and our mind is always under it, no matter how thick of a film there is, there's still empty space, holding the film. Now just like watching clouds pass through the clear blue sky, take notice of what distracts you in your mind, and let it be, like the clouds are let be by the clear blue sky (eventually they disappear).

It's not bad if you keep getting distracted, just open your focus again and notice that you are aware of the thoughts even if you are not going with the trains of thought. You can be aware without having to be invested, just like listening in on a conversation in another room, it's as simple as that.

Step 5. **Detach**. By noticing the distracting thoughts, you are slowly letting them go, because if you just pay attention to them but don't get invested in them, or in other words don't start a train of thought around it, the thoughts will naturally dissipate like clouds, so you don't need to "empty your mind" or "will the thoughts to go away" or any silly things like that.

All your job to do is: see them, notice them, and choose to not attach to them.

Step 6. **Sleep** or **Rest.** Now that you are letting the thoughts pass through you like water and are not paying attention to the form of the water in the cup, you just see the water as it is: it's just water. You can try to sleep in this state and you will pass out very quickly or blackout of, if you want to say it that way. And that's really just it, just purposefully relax and like that you can pass out on purpose to get massive amounts of information poured into your mind the second before you black out. Now do it again. Once you wake back up, and again, and see how every time you close your eyes after having already detached from the thoughts and letting them pass by, the "blackout point" is closer and closer.

Step 7. **See the Self**. In rare instances of this type of "opening your focus" type of meditation many say they experience of strange infinite black void, that can be described as a "3D endless nothingness" and it experienced when one "blacks out" or goes into it through meditation or sleep and does not feel like they have a body anymore. In this state we experience the fundamental nature of the Universe and what Quantum Physicists call the "Unified Field". Many traditions have names for this Nonstate. It is neither here nor there, in or out, self or other, God or Creation, but rather the state of pure pre/post experience (imagine what it would be like to be aware before you were in your mother's womb). Pure and utter infinite nothingness. The Buddhists call it Nirvana (meaning Blown Out), the Toaists call it the great Tao/Dao. Others call it Enlightenment, but I personally believe it is God, or the Self layer of the Mind, underneath all belief systems and frameworks of thinking in a purely present and aware state of "Being" or "Presence". It is in this layer of Mind that ALL exists, every possible experience or expression of Infinity in all times past, present, future, all happening Now. I believe it is the thing that looks through the eyes of all things, and what Alan Watts calls the 'ground of being'. It is in this state of eternal nothingness that the answer to the two most perplexing questions of all history reside: If there is a God, where is it? And: Who Am I?

Step 8. **Experience the Self.** If Everything is happening Now, then to experience it, it must be entered through Nothing, and thus there is no experience that is higher or "more" than the Nothingness and the Love beyond it, and it shines truth on the concept that All is One and that one is I Am.

It is the experience that flashes after the Nothingness that envelopes the mind/body/spirit and can be summarized as Mind/Body/Spirit/Totality. It is the awareness of 'being' all things, everywhere, at all times, in any and all potential expressions, in all possible ways, right here right Now.

This flash of experience is accompanied with an over-whelming sense of Unconditional Infinite Love and is usually like "seeing from the eyes of the Universe", aka experiencing being everything.

Words are but symbols for meaning and there is no language that can accurately describe what I am referring to, but that is okay, because in order to know this truth, one must experience it for him or herself. For there is no other way to prove to you that we are all "it" and "it" is infinite and ever expanding and will never ever not be, for I am that I am, and I Am is you and me, and all of eternity dancing the cosmic dance of form, to be reminded and reawakened to the truth of "I Am".

Quantum Physics already understands that the Universe is Consciousness, and it's the "most advanced science" so until the rest of the world catches up and sees and knows the truth that the "Wave" is Infinite Consciousness and the "Particle" is its creation. And with that you are here and so am I, and so will we be, for all of infinite eternity, doing the same ol' thing, being the Universe, aware of itself.

Chapter 51
There Is Nothing I Am Fighting, Not Even Myself
The Final Chapter

"Once you have tasted flight, you will forever walk the earth with your eyes turned skyward, for there you have been, and there you will always long to return."

— Leonardo da Vinci

Many thousands of years have given humans a rich expression of imagination, many thousands of languages, over four thousand religions and infinite various ways of telling what is right or what is wrong, and we still all have no clue what we are doing.

It's like Earth is an asylum where those who are addicted to belief are dropped and are given complete and absolute free choice of what to believe. Leaving the madhouse patients feeling stranded, cut, thrown in the wind, lost at sea, lost to themselves and worse, not knowing what is wrong. Well what is wrong is that nothing is wrong, and we are all told what is wrong, religion, politics, education, peers, family, environment and even the mind itself, tries to say what is "right" or "wrong" or what is good or bad, what should or shouldn't be done. Yet the insanity that ensues when one does something rather terrible, those that would claim what is "right" or "wrong" call the person a sinner, a criminal, a lunatic, a sociopath, or a mental patient. This is true, relative to the system of belief being used. Well, what system of belief is it that the infinite universe of absolute and utter free will is operated under? Nothing matters, no-thing <u>"matter"s.</u>

What has this book pointed to? Nothingness is the fundamental reality of all things forever and ever and ever. And within this nothingness is everything and everything that will be or ever was or ever wasn't. Does this justify "evil"? No, morals are rather spectacular for karma and point the direction of being a good human. The good thing about religion is it is usually accompanied with hopefully good Morals. Well morals are needed, savagery has no excuse, but does not change that fact that it can happen.

Conscientiousness is morals, compassion is morals, peace is morals, free will and free speech is morals, freedom is and allowing freedom is morals. But to be free and not parasitic to the human race, keep good morals. Do not justify hurting others with morals, do not spend the Self like that. Your creative power is wasted on such mundane fruitless acts of death. This world is already the world of death, do you forget that, You are the world of life. The before and after, the timeless infinite imagination-body of God, expressing through our here creation - the universe.

Take it or leave it, I point to an irrefutable fact: The day to day you is a sand grain in a vast and infinite ocean of Self, and you are both, the Ocean and the Drop/Bobber/Sand grain.

You are the Guide Inside, but the you that you think You are is but a husk of words and stories your mind has recorded as self, experiences reinforcing the stories and causing more and more amnesia. To go into the "blackout point" (The Self level of Subconscious or somewhere in between Theta and Delta) is to go to the place of Remembrance, Heaven, the Kingdom Within, The Dao, Zen, All-that-is, Source, The Universe, The Godhead, Om, Shiva, Brahman, Kali, Infinity, The Allness, The Creator, Allah, God, I Am. All these words are but shadows of an experience far exceeding any and all conceptions only glimpsed by those who open their "doors of perception".

To those less and less rare humans who have "Spiritual Awakenings" or know themselves, not individually, but divinely, I dedicate this to you and all other humans as a seed to shine a light on the Guide Inside and hope that you too *find the guide inside.* For everything you will ever achieve or experience will be an expression of this creative principle, a simple inspired homage to the Self of selfs, the Heart of Hearts, the Soul of Souls, God itself, to God, I pay my respects and thank you personally for writing, reading, and *being* this book, for I know that there is nothing I am fighting not even myself. I and all things, are in Heaven, the Self, absolutely and totally peaceful in our infinity. Ever happy to lend a hand and open the cornucopia of all gifts of the universe to an allowing receiver.

To help you remember, wonder for a moment and imagine what you would feel like if you knew wholeheartedly that "There is nothing I am fighting, not even myself". For that is the absolute self within you, the eternal and absolute peace of the Kingdom Within, Heaven itself, the infinite body of your ever expanding human imagination, the being of God itself - I Am.

Farewell, see you in Everwhen!

"We rode on the winds of the rising storm,

We ran to the sounds of the thunder.

We danced among the lightning bolts,

and tore the world asunder."

— Robert Jordan

Epilogue

You have lived many days and have found many places to be safe amongst the weird and warry of the world. You have found things that only those who dare to stumble into the dark have found and yet splendid wisdom you have found, and brought back a light to transform the base.

Like an alchemist on a vigil, long days and nights have spanned with your searching, and in finding you have done well. But what is to show of what you now know? But a flickering flame or a shadow in a well lit room, to impart what you see, to kindle dreams that correspond to others dreams, you must once again shed what you know and impart the most scantily clad wisdom in recapitulated form.

If you venture to and fro, far and near from peak to summit and share what you hear, everyone, everywhere is doing something similar. Yet everything is so different from village to village, from town to city and state and nation. Every little neighborhood, every little sub culture and microcosmic existence points to that overarching meaning, *to be*.

To be is to die, to die is to live, both changing currents in the world, march progress ever forward. An adage comes to mind "With yesterday dead and gone, all we have is today…" yet to be here today is to be dead of all past trimmings, rid of the husk of last season and day. To emerge from the winter and cocoon of hibernation. To revive like the Kings of Old after the Sun goes down in splendid fashion at the end of the year and with the resurrection of the seasons, the land and people are renewed alike.

The powers of the Sages, the pearls of the Prophets and the Gifts of the Gods all shackle the receivers to their givers. To be free and possessing of these ephemerals is of superb development for the upward path toward the great beyond. Not a single soul will stop changing, but few will experience the supernatural and come back balanced to help guide the rest who are stepping forward.

Given the story of humanity, we are prompt to see our flaws and irredeemability, though the glory of religion is total absolution and from this mire of beliefs we must take the advice of casting off the old, and embracing the newness of blessedness and purity. In energetic terms, we are to be renewed with a new source of energy, the original source of energy, the only source of energy.

Instead of deriving existence from reflections and shards of broken mirrors laid on foundations of antiquity, we take what we see as helpful for our journey and leave the rest. This requires that discernment be fine tuned, for who can possibly know what is right or good for themselves if they do not know what is wrong, harmful or of over self service. In this culling of beliefs and refining of mind and character, we become amalgamated and "whole" psychologically.

What Carl Jung would call, individuated or what Mazlow would call self-actualized. The trek of shedding the skins of belief can be hasty or a prolonged lull into the river of multiplicity, the river of conflicting systems, and the river of doubt. An overdue warning is meant to be here, a warning of "Do Not Stay Too Long or You May Become Lost". But lost, where?

Or is it you that you lose? In searching for what is essential and real, what is true and lasting, all you find is more layers to peel away. Like the Mundaka Upanishad, Mundaka meaning "peeling away" refers to peeling away of the layers of "this or that".

Who is to blame for this quagmire? Certainly not Divinity, the Lord God, the Universe or whatever name you put to it, for the essence of our search is aimed towards that beginningless and endless state. Who can blame the mad for having walked into a place where Pandoras box has well and truly run its course. All of the "pleroma" revealed itself to them in its splendid form yet they live here in this world attempting to function as people. Yet in a different age or a different culture they may have been soothsayers or witch doctors.

The total state of the world is hard to conceive, for the total state of the human condition is sparsely the same but in their similarities we find a hurdle in societal advancement, that being equilibrium of outer and inner needs, of societal infrastructure and of individual meaning and place. Where does this leave us in the world? We are here but not here, and the world is here, but not here. How can we reconcile the changing of the world screen with the changelessness of the Eternal Dream. We can help others around us, and hopefully that help extends to improve the nations in which we reside.

There have been many wars for many reasons, and many places ravaged by differing beliefs to come back a century later and be brothers and sisters. Yet span some more time and they are back to square one. The simple mistakes that are natural to our societal amnesia and our short sighted not learning the lessons of history path, how can we ever hope to be a high civilization again.

With the emergence of more and more advanced Artificial Intelligence we can glimpse where we are headed, when the dystopian dreams are cast aside, we can see that the world is actually headed to a miraculous place. A place never before experienced, with never before problems and solutions. Who are we today, to judge those of tomorrow as being worse off then we are now, when we could be at the precipice of a new age of splendor.

We can dream hell into this world with our dystopian scenes or we can strive to create a world that is one we are all proud to live in. One where we do not collectively feel the need for absolution. A world where the average person sees the glory of the world and does not feel trapped to meaninglessness and hopelessness.

We can do it together with new technology and a new openness to healing ourselves from ourselves. The inner and outer world is changing to be something unrecognizable. A place people have dreamed of for millennia. Our technology will soon be indistinguishable from magic. With a far enough gap, we will be doing things never thought of. Learning to balance ourselves with Nature and at the same time taking quantum leaps.

The planet is undergoing a great change currently where governments are consolidating power and the people are consolidating faith in hope and distrust in government. The place we are in is a masterpiece of moving parts of science, social engineering, and mixing views of the future of culture and religion combined.

For many people life doesn't involve religion, and doesn't need to either. But for a great many more, religion is an absolute bedrock in their life and those many people are in many influential roles and thus the development of our world is linked with the Belief in God or Divinity.

We must see our fellow humans in this light to understand where we are headed. Holiness and Morality are goals and potential realities and are an aim for cultural rehabilitation. I do believe that solid moral truths are important and that this would serve our world.

Some people believe a nefarious group of people rule this planet and are purposefully corralling humanity into a bottleneck and in some ways this is true but we have always had an overweighing support for hope and life than tyranny and destruction. There are bad actors and bad groups and bad plans but those do not encompass the total sum of what exists here on this planet. There is an emergence of good will and striving for the betterment of all of humanity and many more people than you think are working towards this in small ways that all contribute day by day.

To cull populations, cultures and peoples is easy, but to cull the flame inside the heart of humanity is impossible. We have not survived up to this point in time without a tenacity and fortitude that nothing and no one can take. All will try and all will fail to kill the unkillable and sink the unsinkable, we stand on our bedrock and hold our faith because in the darkest night we are preparing for the brightest day.

Save for the fools, we all know what is true, we are to see some rough patches but humanity and spirit will win, humanity and spirit will prosper. All of our world will be unified in peace and harmony eventually. We are to live in the best time to ever exist. The best place in history to be. We are living in the beginning and the end, the birth, death and rebirth and nothing will stop the gears of change.

The indomitable spirit of life proceeds at all costs forward, ever forward and ever upward towards higher peaks and deeper insights. The light of inspiration is to shine more brilliantly than ever before and we are here to witness it.

Appendix

On the Miraculous Workings, Results and Fruits Of Hypnosis & Mesmerism Under Different Names Mystical and Scientific Alike

Section I

"By the expression Animal Magnetism I mean one of the universal operations of Nature, the action of which, when directed on our nerves, offers a universal means of curing and preserving man."

— Franz Anton Mesmer 1771

Hypnosis as we know it is usually thought of as a fringe or quack medicine and therapy type only sought as an absolute last resort for some habit or mental block to be removed. It is shrouded in a mantle of the dark arts and it often invokes the emotion of helpness fear with the concept of being "taken over", "controlled" or "willed" to do something totally and completely against one's wishes. Now mind you all of these things are possible and have happened on many occasions but the overarching results of this art and practice are of a benign and serviceful nature.

Hypnosis as we know was re-pioneered by the famous Franz Anton Mesmer who through many displays of "Animal Magnetism" demonstrated various corrections of ailments and difficulties. So much so that the King Louis XVI of France appointed four members of the Faculty of Medicine to investigate Mesmer's claims of a "Magnetic Fluid" that he deemed to be the universal panacea. This being a very redacted account the results were that they could not find concrete evidence proving his claim of the existence of this etheric fluid, though, they did acknowledge the validity of his patients being cured and simply couldn't come to a conclusion about results in the physical and empirically driven scientific world being brought about by an imaginary substance which has no way of being measured or seen.

This story points to a very important fact in our work here and that fact is simple:

With physical reactions being limited to physical causes we must dismiss almost all facts of how things actually come to pass.

We can conclude our section on Mesmer with the understanding that if we limit our scope of reality to the physical and eliminate all electromagnetism, all psychosomatic, all psychoimmunology and all "energetic" and psychical (emotional and mental) causes whether true or false of health, wellness, accomplishment of goals and all things under heaven as being only and entirely dependant upon physical causes and thus physical effects we stump our human potential and thus kill all progress to be made in the future in terms of technological, spiritual, personal and medical advancement.

Section II

Many things are possible with hypnosis. It is possible to increase and decrease the heart rate, to increase or reduce inflammation, to numb or sensitize the body, to dilate the eyes, to reduce blood pressure, to cause lethargy or catalepsy, to blind, to deaf, to take taste and many, many more things.

Some of these fall into the category of "hallucination" which they can be perceived to be, though, when looked at from the quantum perspective, the interaction of electrons is the answer to which we go. To take sight we simply change the electrons in the eyes, though traditionally it is thought that we simply cause the patient to see nothing or blackness. But if looked at in this quantum perspective we do not only suggest to the patient but we also have an effect on reality itself. The explanation of this is not here and we do not claim to be able to prove it, though it is demonstrable.

The "production" of chemicals from the vast store houses of our epigenetic banks and also the stimulation of specific nerve and hormone centers through suggestion can produce "miraculous" effects. The detailed work of Joe Dispenza titled Becoming Supernatural is an extensive dive into this field.

The suggestion to produce "Metatonin" which is supposedly the sleep paralysis chemical when given to a subject who has no foreknowledge of such a name will nonetheless produce the effect of complete and total paralysis. My personal explanation of this is the Superconscious Mind which has memory of all past and future events and information though to explain and prove this is a stretch.

Now if we see the implication here, we see that all of humanity possesses the memory of all of the rest of humanity and also to a fine degree of refinement the abilities of so-called miracleworkers. The only requisite being a trance on self or other.

The college or club hypnosis show is fine and dandy but when one clears away a lifetime's worth of trauma which also clears away arthritis or thyroid problems or bladder issues and even diseases and syndromes, then there has to be something immense at work.

Section III

The miracles of healing and health have been shown, it is to the opposite we now venture. Here is an excerpt from Eliphas Levi's *"La Clef des grands mystères"* where a woman is paid to be put under trance to be experimented on. Now before you read I issue you a warning that it is possible that what you are about to read is not true but I believe it is because of the nature of spiritual energy and what we have already seen.

Many mediums and seers have been employed by "Magnetisers" (Hypnotists) to use or harness their extrasensory perception to commune with or see other worlds and or beings. Without further adieu here is the story of a woman who was told to see God, Paradise and Hell:

"Certain persons who doubted religion and magnetism at the same

time, those incredules who are ready for all the superstitions and all the fanaticisms, decided to pay a poor girl in silver to submit to their

experiments. She was of a nervous, impressionable nature, fatigued,

moreover, by the excesses of a more than irregular life, and already

disgusted with existence. She is put to sleep, and commanded to see;

she weeps and argues. They speak to her of God.

... she trembles in

every limb.

'No', she says, 'No, he fills me with dread. I will not look at

him.

'Look. I want you to.'

She opens her eyes; her pupils are dilated; she is terrified.

"What do you see?'

- 'I do not know how to say.. . Oh! Mercy, mercy, awaken me!'

"No, look and say what you see.'

- 'I see a black night in which whirling flashes surround two great

eyes which are rolling around. From these eyes shoot rays which

roll in spirals and which fill all space. Oh! It harms me! Awaken me!'

'No, look

"Where would you have me look now?'

"Look into Paradise.

"No, I may not mount there; the great night takes me back and

causes me to fall.'

"Very well, look into Hell'

At this, the somnambulist shook convulsivelv.

- 'No! No!, she cried, sobbing, 'I will not. I would have vertigo. I

would fall. Oh! Hold me back! Hold me back!'

"No. descend.

Where would you have me descend?'

'Into Hell.'

"But it is horrible! No, no, I will not go there."GO

"Mercy!'

"Go there, I want you to.

The features of the somnambulist became terrible to see. Her

hair stood erect on her head. Her eyes, too widely opened, showed

only the white. Her breast heaved, and let escape a sort of rattle.

*Go there, I want you to', repeated the magnetizer.

"I am there', said the unfortunate between her teeth, and fell

exhausted. Then, she responded no more. Her inert head reclined

on her shoulder. Her arms hung long beside her body. She was

approached. She was touched. An effort was made too late to

awaken her. The crime was accomplished. The girl was dead…"

(The quotation and next paragraph are from the book THE TRAVELLER'S GUIDE TO THE ASTRAL PLANE By Steve Richards)

Levi says that 'the authors of this sacrilegious experiment.. were not

pursued' because of 'public incredulity in matters of magnetism ...

The authorities wrote out a death certificate, and it was attributed to the

rupture of an aneurism. The body carried moreover no sign of violence.

It was interred, and everything had been said.' "

Now the authenticity of this is questionable but the message is clear, we have connection to the great beyond and with our interaction with it, there can be effects on us, positive and negative.

There are actually a great many psychologists who have dealt with patients who believe themselves to be possessed or tormented by demons. So many that there are specialists in this type of Psychotherapy. Now the answer to me of why they experience what they do is simple: the highly charged mental and emotional or in other words psychical environment of these "patients" attracts on finer levels of reality those things called spirits, guides, demons and angels…etc.

Section IV

The stimulated brains of these more "sensitive" individuals have a higher concentration of right-brain and whole brain coherency rendering the Reason less powerful and asserting the ephemeral quality of dream and trance experiences. The effect of a more stimulated Pineal Gland and experience of different brainwave states can create such strange experiences that many question their sanity after, especially if they are of a more left brained and "worldly" propensity.

Here enters the enigmatic "Spirit Molecule" also known as Dimethyltryptamine or DMT for short which has fascinated many in recent years and has been proposed to be a "Chemical Doorway" or "Interdimensional Portal".

Weather produced endogenously (through breathwork or meditation etc) or taken exogenously (smoked, drank or IV) the DMT "flash" often resembles that of Near-Death-Experiences, mystical "God" encounters, sleep paralysis episodes, deja vu flashes, deep hypnotic trance and the wonderful experience of Astral Projection.

The beings of light, states of consciousness and overwhelming sensations and feelings of Forgiveness, Gratitude, Wholeness, Love, Vastness or Nothingness etc, are so common and such a shared experience that there has to be some meaning to it. People from many different backgrounds having the same or similar experiences without ever hearing about or experiencing something similar is beyond explanation. The only answer to me is that we as humanity have a greater connection to everything and ourselves then we could possibly ever understand.

The Tibetan Lamas describing from their deep meditations the same places that psychonauts experiencing DMT describe is fascinating, a University mapping out that "realm" because people have so many "same" experiences is amazing but people without taking the psychedelic and experiencing it themselves and activating it inside themselves to go into states of consciousness that mirror what is described in various Holy Books and to experience this regularly and with so many people experiencing seems impossible but it can only mean one thing, this is fundamental and it is natural. It is something that many humans lost because of conditioning, but it is not totally lost.

www.ingramcontent.com/pod-product-compliance
Lightning Source LLC
Chambersburg PA
CBHW061447150726
47987CB00001B/366